Contents

Preface

This workbook has been written to help you in your further understanding of chemistry for the Cambridge IGCSE specification. This workbook should be used alongside the 3rd edition of the IGCSE Chemistry textbook, written by the same authors.

In this workbook the chapters have the same names as those in the textbook and are organised by syllabus topic. They contain questions related to the content of the equivalent chapters in the IGCSE Chemistry textbook. The questions may be related to:

- the 'core' of the IGCSE syllabus
- both the 'core' and the 'extended' parts of the syllabus. If you are to be entered for the extension paper you should try to do these questions as well as the extended questions.
- the 'extended' part of the IGCSE syllabus, which is examined in the extension paper.

Chapter 16 has questions that relate to the 'Alternative to Practical' examination paper.

To ensure your answers to the questions are kept together in one place, there are spaces provided in this book for you to write your answers in. This will help when you come to revise for examinations.

Bryan Earl and Doug Wilford

1 The particulate nature of matter

● Core

1 A sample of a solid substance, which had been cooled to –5 °C, was put into a test-tube.
   The test-tube was then heated in a water bath. The temperature of the substance was taken every
   5 minutes for an hour. The results obtained are shown below.

Time/min	0	5	10	15	20	25	30	35	40	45	50	55	60
Temperature/°C	–5	–1	5	5	7	13	28	45	62	76	79	82	82

a Plot the results on the graph paper below, putting time on the horizontal axis and temperature
   on the vertical axis.

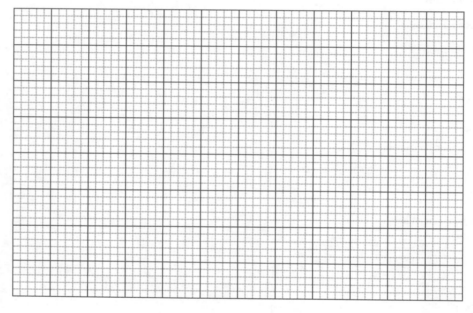

[4]

b What is the melting point of the substance? .... [1]

c What is the boiling point of the substance? .... [1]

d Describe what is happening to the particles of the substance after 50 minutes.

....

.... [2]

2 Imagine that you are a water molecule in an ice cube. Describe what happens to you as the ice cube is heated up to a temperature of 100 °C.

....

....

....

.... *[6]*

3 a Explain the meaning of each of the following terms.

    i melting .... *[1]*   iv condensation .... *[1]*

    ii chemical change .... *[1]*   v evaporation .... *[1]*

    iii sublimation .... *[1]*   vi dissolving .... *[1]*

  b Which of the terms given in part **a** best describes what is taking place in each of the following?

    i The formation of water droplets on the inside of a window on a cold day.

      .... *[1]*

    ii The formation of liquid potassium chloride from solid potassium chloride

      using strong heat. .... *[1]*

    iii The formation of iodine vapour from solid iodine on heating. .... *[1]*

    iv Adding sugar to hot coffee to sweeten the drink. .... *[1]*

● Core/Extended

4 Use ideas about kinetic theory to explain the following:

  a Diffusion does not occur in solids.

....

.... *[2]*

  b Gases can be compressed more than liquids.

....

.... *[2]*

  c It is possible for a liquid to flow but a solid cannot.

....

.... *[2]*

● Extended

5 When the following experiment is set up, a cloud of fine white powder can be seen as the ammonia gas reacts with the hydrogen chloride gas.

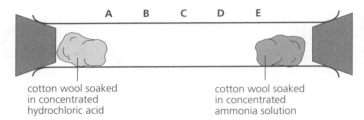

cotton wool soaked
in concentrated
hydrochloric acid

cotton wool soaked
in concentrated
ammonia solution

Hydrogen chloride particles are more than twice as heavy as ammonia particles.

a   Which of the particles will move faster? .... [1]

b   At which point, **A** to **E**, along the tube will the white cloud be seen? Explain your answer in terms of the movement of the particles.

.... [2]

c   How do the particles of hydrogen chloride and ammonia gas move along the tube?

.... [1]

Exam focus

1   a   i   Give two properties shown by:

a solid .... [2]

a liquid .... [2]

a gas. .... [2]

ii   Draw diagrams in the boxes below to show how the particles are arranged in each of the physical states.

  solid   **liquid**   **gas**   [3]

b   The melting and boiling points of five substances are given in the table.

(Take room temperature as 298 K.)

Substance	Melting point/K	Boiling point/K
Oxygen	55	90
Bromine	266	332
Mercury	234	630
Phosphorus	317	553
Iron	1808	3023

    i   What is the melting point of mercury in °C? ....   *[1]*

    ii Which element/s is a gas at room temperature? ....   *[1]*

    iii Which element/s is a solid at room temperature? ....   *[1]*

    iv Which of the elements will boil first if the temperature is raised from room

    temperature? ....   *[1]*

[Total: 13]

2 Use the kinetic theory to explain the following.

    a Walking along the street in front of a coffee shop, it is possible to smell the coffee.

    ....

    ....   *[2]*

    b When laying railway track, gaps have to be left between the lengths of track.

    ....

    ....   *[2]*

    c When a tea bag is placed in a cup of hot water, the colour of the water changes.

    ....

    ....   *[2]*

    d In cold weather, the amount of water found running down the inside of windows increases.

    ....

    ....   *[2]*

    e A bubble of methane rises from the bottom of the Pacific Ocean. As it rises, the bubble gets bigger.

    ....

    ....

    ....   *[2]*

    f Pollen grains are mixed with water and observed under a microscope. Dust particles in the air are also observed in the same way.

      i   What would the pollen grains and dust particles be doing?

      ....   *[1]*

      ii What causes the grains and dust particles to behave in the way you have described in part **i**?

      ....

      ....   *[2]*

[Total: 13]

Elements, compounds and experimental techniques

(2)

● Core

1 The table below shows the melting points, boiling points and densities of elements **A** to **E**.

Substance	Melting point/°C	Boiling point/°C	Density/g cm^{-3}
A	−259	−253	0.09
B	1085	2580	8.93
C	−7	59	3.1
D	−39	357	13.6
E	−218	−183	0.0013

a Which of these substances, **A** to **E**, are gases at room temperature? .... [2]

b Which of these substances, **A** to **E**, are liquids at room temperature? .... [2]

c Which of these substances, **A** to **E**, are solids at room temperature? .... [1]

d Which **two** of these substances, **A** to **E**, are most likely to be metals? .... [2]

e Which of these substances, **A** to **E**, is most likely to be mercury? .... [1]

f Which of these substances, **A** to **E**, is the least dense metal? .... [1]

g Which of these substances, **A** to **E**, will be a liquid at −210 °C? .... [1]

2 a Pick the 'odd one out' in each of the following groups of elements and explain why it is different from the others.

    i Cu, C, Ca, Cs, Cr

       Odd one out ....

       Explanation .... [2]

    ii nitrogen, neon, sulfur, iron, silicon

       Odd one out ....

       Explanation .... [2]

    iii Mg, Al, Cl, Na, Ar

       Odd one out ....

       Explanation .... [2]

b For each of the following statements about elements, write either 'true' or 'false'.

  i   There are only 103 elements. .... [1]

  ii   More elements are metals than non-metals. .... [1]

  iii Each element has a chemical name and a symbol. .... [1]

  iv   Metals such as magnesium contain two atoms joined together to form molecules.

       .... [1]

  v   Molecules of argon contain only one atom. .... [1]

  vi   Some of the symbols for the elements come from their Chinese names. .... [1]

  vii Where elements contain two atoms joined together in pairs, they are called diatomic.

       .... [1]

3 a Distinguish between the terms *compound* and *mixture*, using specific examples.

   ....

   ....

   .... [3]

   b Here is a list of substances:

   | stainless steel   carbon monoxide   lemonade   sulfuric acid   cement |
   | methane   sodium hydroxide   limestone   beer   brass |

   Which of these substances are:

   i   compounds? .... [5]

   ii   mixtures? .... [5]

   c Pick the 'odd one out' in each of the following groups and explain why it is different from the others.

   i   petrol, oil, water, air, solder

        Odd one out ....

        Explanation .... [2]

   ii   lead nitrate, potassium oxide, chromium, hydrochloric acid, silicon dioxide

        Odd one out ....

        Explanation .... [2]

   iii HCl, F_2, MgO, FeS, CO_2

        Odd one out ....

        Explanation .... [2]

4 a A mixture of zinc metal powder and sulfur was heated strongly in a test-tube. A bright red glow spread very quickly throughout the mixture during the reaction. At the end of the experiment, a white powder was produced.

   i   What safety precautions should be taken when carrying out this experiment?

   .... *[2]*

   ii Explain what the 'bright red glow' indicates. .... *[1]*

   iii Give the chemical name of the 'white powder'. .... *[1]*

   iv Write a word equation and a balanced chemical equation for the reaction that has taken place.

   ....

   ....

   .... *[3]*

   v   The white solid is a compound. Explain the difference between the mixture of zinc and sulfur and the compound formed by the chemical reaction between them.

   ....

   ....

   .... *[3]*

   vi Many compounds are very useful substances. Salt (chemical name sodium chloride) is one of these useful compounds. It is a white crystalline solid and has been prized by people for a very long time. Find and make a list of some things that we use salt for in our world today.

   ....

   .... *[3]*

   b The metal copper can be extracted from its ore, copper sulfide, in a two-stage process:

   I   Copper sulfide reacts with oxygen at a high temperature to form copper oxide and sulfur dioxide gas.

   II Then the copper oxide is reacted with carbon, again at high temperature, to form copper metal and carbon dioxide gas.

   i   Name the elements mentioned in the passage above.

   .... *[3]*

   ii Name the compounds mentioned in the passage above.

   .... *[4]*

   iii Write word and balanced chemical equations for the reactions described in the passage above.

   ....

   ....

   ....

   .... *[8]*

5 a The table below shows the formulae for some compounds.

Complete the table by writing in:

   i the symbols present in each formula and the elements they represent [12]

   ii the number of atoms of each element present in the formula [12]

   iii the total number of atoms present in the formula. [4]

The first one has been done for you.

Formula of substance	Elements present			Total number of atoms
	Symbol	Name	Number of atoms	
$LiNO_3$	Li	Lithium	1	5
	N	Nitrogen	1	
	O	Oxygen	3	
$CaCO_3$				
Mg_3N_2				
Ag_2CrO_4				
$AlBr_4Cs$				

b Balance the following equations. Some of the spaces should be left blank.

   i ....$Pb(s)$ + ...$O_2(g)$ → ....$PbO(s)$ [2]

   ii ....$H_2(g)$ + ...$O_2(g)$ → ....$H_2O(l)$ [2]

   iii ....$C_2H_4(g)$ + ...$O_2(g)$ → ....$CO_2(g)$ + ...$H_2O(l)$ [2]

   iv ....$Fe(s)$ + ...$Br_2(l)$ → ....$FeBr_3(s)$ [2]

   v ....$CuO(s)$ + ...$HCl(aq)$ → ....$CuCl_2(aq)$ + ...$H_2O(l)$ [2]

   vi ....$SnO_2(s)$ + ...$H_2(g)$ → ....$Sn(s)$ + ...$H_2O(l)$ [2]

6 a The diagram on the right shows the apparatus used for fractional distillation. The labels have been replaced with numbers.

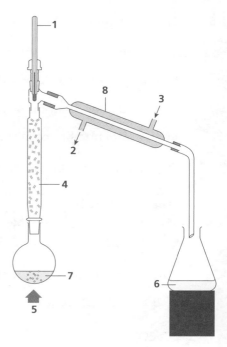

i For each number, write down the correct label from the list below.

Liebig condenser	fractionating column
cold water out	distillate	cold water in
thermometer	mixture of liquids	heat

1 .... *[1]*

2 .... *[1]*

3 .... *[1]*

4 .... *[1]*

5 .... *[1]*

6 .... *[1]*

7 .... *[1]*

8 .... *[1]*

ii Which of the following mixtures can be separated successfully by fractional distillation? Explain your answers.

| crude oil | magnesium and sulfur | a mixture of dyes | air |

....

....

.... *[4]*

b The diagram on the right shows a simple apparatus used for chromatography. The labels have been replaced with numbers.
For each number, write down the correct label from the list in the box.

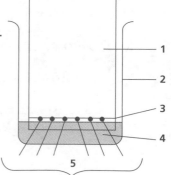

| pencil line | beaker | solvent | samples |
| chromatography paper |

1 .... *[1]*   4 .... *[1]*

2 .... *[1]*   5 .... *[1]*

3 .... *[1]*

c   What do you understand by the term *accuracy of experimental work*?

....

.... [2]

d   Which of the following are units of:

   i   time ....

   ii   temperature ....

   iii   volume ....

   iv   mass ....

cm³   kilograms   hours   degrees Celsius   litres   minutes   seconds   grams

[8]

e   In experiments you will require the use of accurate measuring instruments. What accuracy would you expect of:

   i   a stopwatch .... [1]   iii   an electronic balance .... [1]

   ii   a thermometer .... [1]   iv   a burette .... [1]

● Extended

7   The metal zinc can be extracted from its ore, zinc sulfide (zinc blende), in a two-stage process. The second part of the process involves a *redox* reaction in which zinc oxide is reacted with carbon, at a high temperature, to form zinc metal and carbon monoxide gas.

   zinc oxide + coke (carbon) → zinc + carbon monoxide

a   What do you understand by the term *redox?*

.... [2]

b   Which of the substances shown in the word equation is being:

   i   oxidised? .... [1]   ii   reduced? .... [1]

c   Which of the substances shown in the word equation is acting as the:

   i   oxidising agent? .... [1]   ii   reducing agent? .... [1]

d   Write a balanced chemical equation for the reaction shown in the word equation.

.... [2]

e   The word equations below describe reactions by which the metals lead and tin are obtained from their ores.

lead oxide + carbon → lead + carbon dioxide

tin(IV) oxide + hydrogen gas → tin + water

In each of these reactions, which of the substances shown is being:

i   oxidised? .... [2]   ii   reduced? .... [2]

Which of the substances shown is acting as the:

iii oxidising agent? .... [2]   iv reducing agent? .... [2]

v   Write a balanced chemical equation for each of these reactions.

....

.... [6]

Exam focus

Core

1   The table below shows some information about four different elements, W, X, Y and Z. (Note that W, X, Y and Z are *not* chemical symbols.)

a   Complete the following table.

Element	Metal or non-metal?	Shiny?	Conductor of electricity?	Melting point
W	Metal		Yes	High
X	Non-metal	No	No	Low
Y		Yes	Yes	High
Z	Non-metal	No		Low

[3]

b   Zinc is a metal. Give **one** property of zinc, *not shown in the table,* which shows that it is a metal.

.... [1]

c   Sparklers are a type of firework. They usually consist of a chemical mixture that has been moulded onto a thin wire. One of the main substances found in the mixture is iron powder.

The word equation for one of the main reactions that takes place during the burning of a sparkler is:

iron + oxygen → iron oxide

i   Give the name of one of the *reactants* present in the word equation above. .... [1]

ii   Give the name of the *compound* present in the word equation above. .... [1]

iii Give **one** reason why people should be careful when handling sparklers.

.... [1]

   iv Write a balanced chemical equation for the reaction of iron with oxygen.

.... [3]

[Total: 10]

Core/Extended

2 Iron is usually extracted from its ore haematite (iron(III) oxide). The following is a brief outline of the reactions involved in this extraction.

  I   coke + oxygen → carbon dioxide

  II carbon dioxide + coke → carbon monoxide

  III iron(III) oxide + carbon monoxide → iron + carbon dioxide

  a Write balanced chemical equations for:

    i   reaction I .... [2]

    ii reaction II. .... [3]

  b Which substance is being oxidised in reaction I? .... [1]

  c Which substance is being reduced in reaction II? .... [1]

  d Balance the following equation for reaction III. Some spaces may be left blank.

    .... $Fe_2O_3(s)$ + ... $CO(g)$ → .... $Fe(l)$ + ... $CO_2(g)$ [2]

  e In reaction III, which substance is acting as the reducing agent and which is acting as

    the oxidising agent? .... [2]

  f Complete the table below.

Formula of substance	Elements present			Total number of atoms
	Name	Symbol	Number of atoms	
Fe_2O_3				
CO				
Fe				
CO_2				

[25]

  g Which of the substances shown in the table are:

    i   elements? ....

    ii compounds? .... [4]

[Total: 40]

Atomic structure and bonding

• Core

1 Complete the following table.

Element	Atomic number	Mass number	Number of protons	Number of electrons	Number of neutrons	Electron configuration
A	5	11				
B		24	12			
C		39				2,8,8,1
D					20	2,8,8,2

[16]

2 For each of the following statements about ionic/covalent bonding and ionic/covalent compounds, write either 'true' or 'false'.

a Ionic bonds are formed between non-metals only. .... [1]

b Ionic bonds are formed by transfer of electrons between the elements forming the bond.

.... [1]

c Ionic compounds usually have low melting points and high boiling points. .... [1]

d Covalent bonds are formed between non-metals only. .... [1]

e Covalent bonds are formed by sharing of electrons between the elements forming the bond.

.... [1]

f Covalent compounds usually have low melting and boiling points. .... [1]

3 The diagrams below show two different forms of carbon, **A** and **B**.

A

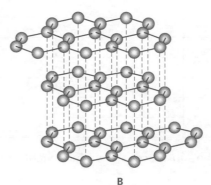

B

a Name the two allotropes of carbon shown above. .... [2]

b Explain the meaning of the term *allotrope*.

.... [2]

c i What type of bonding is represented by these forms of carbon? .... [1]

  ii What type of structure is represented by these forms of carbon? .... [1]

d i How many other carbon atoms are linked to each carbon atom in form **A**? .... [1]

  ii How many other carbon atoms are linked to each carbon atom in form **B**? .... [1]

e Complete the table below, which relates to the properties of the metal copper and substances **A** and **B**.

Substance	Electrical conductivity	Melting point	Hardness
Copper	Good	High	High
A			
B			

[6]

f In 1985, a new allotrope of carbon was discovered. What is the name of this allotrope?

.... [1]

● Core/Extended

4 Draw diagrams to show the bonding in each of the following ionic compounds.

a lithium chloride (LiCl)

[4]

b calcium sulfide (CaS)

[4]

5   a   The table shows the valencies of some common ions. Use the information in the table to work
         out the formula of each of the compounds listed below.

	Valency (oxidation state)		
	1	**2**	**3**
Metals	Sodium (Na^+) Potassium (K^+) Silver (Ag^+)	Magnesium (Mg^{2+}) Lead (Pb^{2+}) Barium (Ba^{2+}) Copper (Cu^{2+})	Aluminium (Al^{3+}) Iron (Fe^{3+})
Non-metals	Fluoride (F^-) Chloride (Cl^-) Bromide (Br^-)	Oxide (O^{2-}) Sulfide (S^{2-})	
Groups of atoms	Hydroxide (OH^-) Nitrate (NO_3^-) Ammonium (NH_4^+)	Carbonate (CO_3^{2-}) Sulfate (SO_4^{2-})	Phosphate (PO_4^{3-})

i   potassium chloride .... [1]   vi   ammonium sulfate .... [1]

ii   copper(II) fluoride .... [1]   vii   magnesium phosphate .... [1]

iii sodium carbonate .... [1]   viii barium sulfide .... [1]

iv   silver phosphate .... [1]   ix   aluminium hydroxide .... [1]

v   lead oxide .... [1]   x   iron(III) bromide .... [1]

b   Using the formulae from your answers to part **a**, give the ratio of the atoms present for each of
    those compounds.

i   .... [1]   vi   .... [1]

ii   .... [1]   vii   .... [1]

iii .... [1]   viii .... [1]

iv   .... [1]   ix   .... [1]

v   .... [1]   x   .... [1]

6   Draw diagrams to show the bonding in each of the following covalent compounds.

    a   hydrogen fluoride (HF)

[4]

b   nitrogen trichloride (NCl$_3$)

[4]

● Extended

7   a   The bonding in metals can be described in the following way:

'It is an electrostatic force of attraction between free electrons and the regular array of positive metal ions within the solid metal. The bonding in metals gives rise to certain properties.'

Complete the following passage about the properties of metals by writing in words from the list.

| energy levels   ductile   energy   attractive   delocalised |
| high   malleable   ions   conductors   negative |

Metals are good .... of electricity and heat, because the free electrons from

the outer .... of metal atoms carry a ....

charge or heat .... through the metal. The free electrons are often described as

.... The free electrons allow metal .... to slide over each other, so metals

are .... and .... They have .... melting and boiling points

due to the strong .... forces within the structure of the metal.   [10]

b   The melting point of calcium (840 °C) is much higher than that of potassium (63 °C).
Using the idea of metallic bonding, explain why this is the case.

....

....

....

....   [4]

Exam focus

Core

1 One of our most important fuels is natural gas (methane, CH_4). The diagram below shows the bonding in a methane molecule.

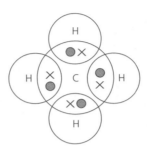

a What type of bonding is shown in this methane molecule? .... [1]

b What type of particle is represented by the dots and crosses? .... [1]

c Methane is a gas at room temperature and pressure. Explain why this is the case.

....

.... [2]

d Why are four hydrogen atoms needed for each carbon atom in the methane molecule?

....

.... [2]

e i What inert (noble) gas structure do the hydrogen atoms have? .... [1]

ii What inert (noble) gas structure does the carbon atom have? .... [1]

iii When atoms within a molecule form chemical bonds, they normally end up with eight electrons in their outer energy level. Why do the hydrogen atoms have only two?

....

.... [1]

[Total: 9]

Extended

2 The diagram below shows the structure of sodium chloride (salt).

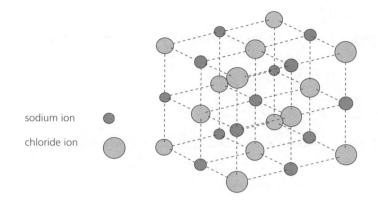

sodium ion

chloride ion

a How does the electronic structure of a sodium atom differ from that of a sodium ion?

.... *[2]*

b How does the electronic structure of a chlorine atom differ from that of a chloride ion?

.... *[2]*

c What type of chemical bond is found in sodium chloride? .... *[1]*

d Using the diagram of sodium chloride above, explain why sodium chloride:

 i forms crystals that are cubic in shape

   ....

   .... *[2]*

 ii has a high melting point (801 °C)

   ....

   .... *[2]*

 iii acts as an insulator when solid, but will conduct electricity when molten.

   ....

   .... *[2]*

[Total: 11]

Stoichiometry – chemical calculations

Use the Periodic Table on page 2 to look up any values for relative atomic mass that you may need in this chapter.

● Core

1 a Calculate the relative molecular mass of each of the following compounds.

i C_2H_5OH .... *[1]*   iii CH_3CH_2COOH .... *[1]*

ii $CH_3COOCH_2CH_3$ .... *[1]*   iv CH_3CH═CH_2 .... *[1]*

b Calculate the relative formula mass of each of the following compounds.

i Na_2CO_3 .... *[1]*   iii $(NH_4)_2SO_4$ .... *[1]*

ii $Ca(OH)_2$ .... *[1]*   iv Fe_2O_3 .... *[1]*

● Core/Extended

2 A student carried out a reaction between iron and hydrochloric acid to make some iron(II) chloride crystals. She started with 5.6 g of iron and used an excess of hydrochloric acid.

a i Write a balanced chemical equation for the reaction.

.... *[3]*

ii How many moles of iron did she start off with?

.... *[1]*

iii What mass of iron(II) chloride could she have expected to obtain from this reaction?

.... *[2]*

iv She actually obtained 9.17 g of the iron(II) chloride. What was her percentage yield?

.... *[2]*

b Iron is extracted from its ore haematite (Fe_2O_3) in the blast furnace. The reaction that produces the iron is:

$Fe_2O_3(s) + 3CO(g) \rightarrow 2Fe(s) + 3CO_2(g)$

100 tonnes of haematite gave 7 tonnes of iron. Calculate the percentage yield of the process.

....

.... *[4]*

● Extended

3 a Calculate the number of moles of the element in:

   i 54 g of aluminium .... [1]   ii 0.4 g of calcium .... [1]

   b Calculate the number of moles of the compound in:

   i 51 g of aluminium oxide (Al_2O_3) .... [1]   ii 116 g of butane (C_4H_{10}) .... [1]

4 Calculate the mass of:

   a 2 moles of calcium carbonate .... [1]

   b 0.25 mole of water .... [1]

   c 2.5 moles of sodium hydroxide. .... [1]

5 a Calculate the empirical formulae of the compounds with the following compositions by mass.

   i 24.0 g of calcium and 5.6 g of nitrogen   ii 50.8 g of copper and 6.4 g of oxygen

   .... [2]   .... [2]

   iii 2.18 g of carbon, 0.36 g of hydrogen and 1.46 g of oxygen

   .... [2]

   b Calculate the empirical formulae of the compounds with the following percentage compositions by mass.

   i 92.3% carbon and 7.7% hydrogen   ii 60.0% magnesium and 40.0% oxygen

   .... [2]   .... [2]

   iii 27.4% sodium, 1.2% hydrogen, 14.3% carbon and 57.1% oxygen

   .... [2]

6 a Calculate the number of moles of solute in each of the following solutions.

    i $0.5 \, dm^3$ of $0.25 \, mol \, dm^{-3}$ NaOH

    .... *[1]*

    ii $100 \, cm^3$ of $0.5 \, mol \, dm^{-3}$ NaCl

    .... *[1]*

  b Calculate the concentration (in $mol \, dm^{-3}$) of each of the following solutions.

    i   0.5 mole of sodium hydroxide in $500 \, cm^3$

    .... *[1]*

    ii 0.25 mole of copper(II) sulfate in $250 \, cm^3$

    .... *[1]*

7 To find out the concentration of a solution of hydrochloric acid, a student carried out a titration. She found that $18.95 \, cm^3$ of the hydrochloric acid was needed to neutralise $25 \, cm^3$ of a $0.1 \, mol \, dm^{-3}$ sodium carbonate solution.

  a Write a balanced chemical equation for the reaction between hydrochloric acid and sodium carbonate.

    .... *[3]*

  b Describe how the titration procedure was carried out.

    ....

    ....

    ....

    .... *[5]*

  c Use the information given to find the concentration of the hydrochloric acid solution.

    ....

    .... *[3]*

8 When sodium chloride reacts with concentrated sulfuric acid, hydrogen chloride gas (HCl) is one of the products.

    $H_2SO_4(l) + NaCl(s) \rightarrow NaHSO_4(s) + HCl(g)$

If hydrogen chloride gas is dissolved in water, a solution of hydrochloric acid is formed. What would be the concentration of the hydrochloric acid obtained if the reaction was carried out using $11.7 \, g$ of sodium chloride, and the hydrogen chloride gas was dissolved in $250 \, cm^3$ of water?

....

.... *[4]*

Exam focus

Extended

1 a Copper(II) oxide can be reduced to copper by passing hydrogen gas over the oxide, as shown in the equation below. A student started the experiment with 8 g of copper(II) oxide and passed hydrogen gas over the heated oxide to produce copper metal.

$CuO(s) + H_2(g) \rightarrow Cu(s) + H_2O(g)$

i What volume of hydrogen gas would be needed to react with all the copper(II) oxide? (1 mole of any gas at room temperature and pressure has a volume of 24 dm³.)

....

....

.... [3]

ii What mass of copper metal could be obtained from this reaction?

....

.... [2]

iii The student obtained 5.8 g of copper. What was his percentage yield?

.... [2]

b The hydrocarbon propane (C_3H_8) undergoes complete combustion as shown by the equation below.

$C_3H_8(g) + 5O_2(g) \rightarrow 3CO_2(g) + 4H_2O(g)$

i What volume of oxygen gas would be needed to react completely with 10 dm³ of propane gas?

....

....

.... [3]

ii What would be the total volume of gases produced from the reaction of propane with 10 dm³ of oxygen?

....

....

.... [3]

[Total: 13]

2   This question is about a titration involving the neutralisation reaction of $25\,cm^3$ of dilute sodium hydroxide with dilute sulfuric acid.

The initial concentration of the dilute sodium hydroxide was $0.25\,mol\,dm^{-3}$. The solution in the burette was dilute sulfuric acid. The indicator used was phenolphthalein. The table shows the titration results.

	Rough	1	2	3
Final burette reading/cm³	21.75	28.25	22.35	27.30
Initial burette reading/cm³	0.00	6.00	0.00	5.00
Volume of sulfuric acid used/cm³				

a   Complete the table by calculating the volume of dilute sulfuric acid used in each titration.   *[1]*

b   From the three most accurate results, calculate the average volume of sulfuric acid used.

.... *[2]*

c   Write a balanced chemical equation for the reaction.

.... *[3]*

d   From the information given, calculate the number of moles of sodium hydroxide in $25\,cm^3$ of solution.

....

.... *[2]*

e   How many moles of sulfuric acid were neutralised?

.... *[1]*

f   Calculate the concentration of the dilute sulfuric acid.

....

.... *[2]*

[Total: 11]

Electricity and chemistry

● Core

1   The table below shows the results of testing a number of solid and liquid substances to see if they conducted an electric current. The electrodes used were made from platinum in each case.

Substance	Physical state	Conductivity	Products
T	Liquid	Yes	Hydrogen and chlorine
U	Liquid	Yes	Silvery metal and green vapour
V	Liquid	No	None
W	Liquid	Yes	Hydrogen and oxygen
X	Liquid	Yes	None
Y	Solid	Yes	None
Z	Liquid	Yes	Pink-brown metal and oxygen

a   Which of these substances, **T** to **Z**, are electrolytes? .... [4]

b   Which of these substances, **T** to **Z**, may be metals? .... [2]

c   Which of these substances, **T** to **Z**, may be sodium chloride? .... [1]

d   Which of these substances, **T** to **Z**, may be mercury? .... [1]

e   Which of these substances, **T** to **Z**, may be sugar solution? .... [1]

f   Give the name of a substance that **W** may be. .... [1]

g   Give the name of a substance that **Z** may be. .... [1]

2   Complete the table below about a series of electrolysis experiments.

Substance	Material of electrodes	Substance formed at the cathode	Substance formed at the anode
Molten lead(II) chloride	Carbon		
	Platinum	Hydrogen	Oxygen
Molten calcium bromide			
		Sodium	Chlorine
Copper(II) sulfate solution	Copper		

[10]

● Core/Extended

3   Explain the following.

   a   In the purification of copper by electrolysis, it is essential that a little dilute sulfuric acid is added
       to the electrolyte.

       .... [1]

   b   In the electrolysis of concentrated sodium chloride solution, it is necessary to keep the chlorine
       gas and sodium hydroxide separated.

       .... [2]

   c   In the extraction of aluminium from aluminium oxide, the anodes are replaced regularly.

       .... [2]

   d   In any electroplating process, it is necessary to degrease the metal to be plated before the process
       is started.

       .... [2]

● Extended

4   Complete and balance the following ionic equations for processes that take place at the electrodes
    during electrolysis.

   a Na^+ + ... $\rightarrow$ Na   [1]

   b   .... Br^- $\rightarrow$ .... + 2e   [2]

   c Ca^{2+} + ... $\rightarrow$ ....   [2]

   d   .... + ... $^-$ $\rightarrow$ Cu   [2]

   e   .... I^- $\rightarrow$ .... + ...   [3]

   f   .... OH^- $\rightarrow$ .... H_2O + ... + ... e^- [4]

5 The diagram below shows an electrolysis cell.

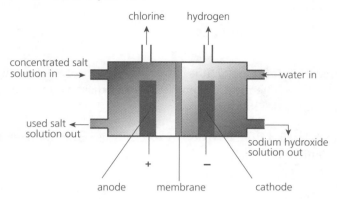

a Name the materials used to make:

   i   the anode .... *[1]*   ii the cathode. .... *[1]*

b i   Hydrogen is produced at the cathode. Balance the following electrode equation for this process. Some spaces may be left blank.

   .... H⁺(aq) + ... e⁻ → .... H₂(g)   *[2]*

   ii Chlorine is produced at the anode. Balance the following electrode equation for this process. Some spaces may be left blank.

   .... Cl⁻(aq) → .... Cl₂ + ... e⁻   *[2]*

   iii Give two large-scale uses for hydrogen and two for chlorine.

   ....

   ....   *[4]*

c The overall chemical equation that represents what is happening in the electrolysis cell shown above is:

   $2NaCl(aq) + 2H_2O(l) \rightarrow 2NaOH(aq) + Cl_2(g) + H_2(g)$

   If 234 g of sodium chloride was electrolysed, calculate the mass of each of the following substances that would be formed. (Ar values: H = 1; O = 16; Na = 23; Cl = 35.5)

   i   sodium hydroxide

   ....   *[2]*

   ii chlorine

   ....   *[2]*

   iii hydrogen

   ....   *[2]*

d Give two large-scale uses for sodium hydroxide.

   ....   *[2]*

Exam focus

Extended

1   Aluminium is an extremely useful metal. It is extracted by electrolysis from its ore, bauxite. Pure aluminium oxide is separated chemically from bauxite and dissolved in molten cryolite. It is then electrolysed in a steel cell lined with carbon.

a   Why is aluminium extracted from its oxide by electrolysis rather than by using a chemical reducing agent such as the element carbon?

....

.... [2]

b   The electrolysis cell operates at about 1000 °C. This is well below the melting point of aluminium oxide, which is 2070 °C. How is the molten state maintained so that electrolysis can take place?

....

.... [2]

c   i   At which electrode is the aluminium produced? .... [1]

ii   Balance the following equation for the depositing of aluminium.

.... Al^{3+} + ... e^- → .... Al [1]

d   i   Oxygen gas is produced at the other electrode. What is this electrode made from?

.... [1]

ii   Balance the following equation for the production of oxygen gas at this electrode.

.... O^{2-} → .... O_2 + ... e^- [2]

e   i   What further chemical reaction takes place at the electrode where oxygen is produced?

....

.... [2]

ii   Write a balanced chemical equation for this reaction.

.... [2]

f   Why are aluminium smelters situated in hilly or mountainous areas?

.... [2]

g   Large amounts of aluminium are recycled. Suggest two advantages of doing this.

....

.... [2]

[Total: 17]

2 Food cans are usually made from mild steel with a thin layer of tin deposited on its surface by electrolysis. A simplified diagram of the electroplating process is shown below.

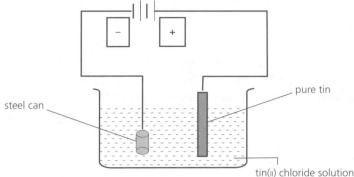

a i How does the mass of the cathode change during the process? .... [1]

  ii Why does the mass of the cathode change?

     .... [1]

b i What charge do the tin ions in the tin(II) sulfate solution carry? .... [1]

  ii How did you decide on your answer to part i?

     .... [1]

c i Does the concentration of the tin(II) sulfate solution differ at the end of the process compared to the beginning? .... [1]

  ii Explain your answer to part i.

     ....

     .... [2]

d i Write a balanced equation for the electrode process that takes place at the cathode for the depositing of tin.

     .... [3]

  ii Write a balanced equation for the electrode process that takes place at the anode.

     .... [3]

e Steel used to be plated by dipping it into molten tin. Why has this method been replaced by electroplating?

     ....

     .... [2]

f Suggest a reason why food cans are made from mild steel electroplated with tin rather than from mild steel alone.

     ....

     .... [1]

[*Total: 16*]

6 Chemical energetics

● Core

1 Crude oil is a very important mixture. There are many substances in this mixture that are used as fuels or as the starting materials for the production of a variety of important chemicals. Oil can be separated by fractional distillation. A simplified diagram of this process is shown below.

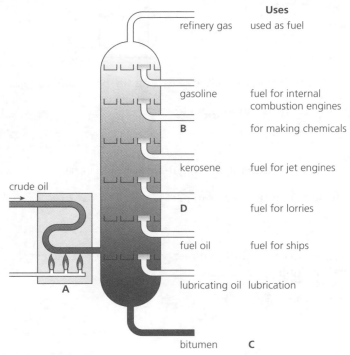

a Why are oil refineries usually found near ports?

.... [1]

b i What change to the crude oil takes place in part **A**?

....

.... [2]

ii Name the fraction **B**. .... [1]

iii Give the use **C**. .... [1]

iv Name the fraction **D**. .... [1]

c Which of the fractions shown in the diagram contains:

i the biggest molecules? .... [1]

ii the smallest molecules? .... [1]

d Which of the fractions represents liquids with the lowest boiling points?

.... [1]

e The gasoline is itself a mixture of substances. How are these different substances separated?

.... [1]

2 a What is a *fuel*?

.... [2]

b Give four properties of a good fuel.

....

.... [4]

c Name:

i a liquid fuel .... [1]

ii a solid fuel .... [1]

iii a gaseous fuel. .... [1]

d Write word and balanced chemical equations for the burning of the gaseous fuel you have named in your answer to part **c iii**.

....

.... [4]

● Extended

3 The reaction between methane and oxygen is exothermic. The standard heat of combustion of methane is $-728 \, kJ \, mol^{-1}$.

$$CH_4(g) + 2O_2(g) \rightarrow CO_2(g) + 2H_2O(l) \qquad \Delta H = -728 \, kJ \, mol^{-1}$$

a Calculate the amount of energy produced when each of the following amounts of methane is completely combusted.

i 2 moles of methane .... [1]

ii 0.25 mole of methane .... [1]

iii 8 g of methane .... [1]

iv 64 g of methane .... [1]

b Draw an energy level diagram to represent the complete combustion of 1 mole of methane.

[3]

4 Use the bond energy data given in the table below to answer this question.

Bond	Bond energy/kJ mol^{-1}
C—H	413
O=O	498
C=O	805
H—O	464
C—C	347

a Calculate the enthalpy of combustion of propane.

$$C_3H_8(g) + 5O_2(g) \rightarrow 3CO_2(g) + 4H_2O(g)$$

....

....

....

....

....

.... [5]

b Draw an energy level diagram to represent this combustion process.

[3]

c How much energy is released when each of the following amounts of propane is burned?
   (A_r values: H = 1; C = 12)

   i   0.5 mole of propane .... [1]

   ii 5 moles of propane .... [1]

   iii 11 g of propane .... [1]

5 Water is formed and energy is released when hydrogen combines with oxygen.

a Write a balanced chemical equation, including state symbols, for this reaction.

.... [4]

b In this reaction, the covalent bonds in the molecules of hydrogen and oxygen are broken. Is the bond breaking process exothermic or endothermic? Explain your answer.

....

.... [2]

c Use the bond energies in the table below to calculate the energy change for the reaction you have shown in part **a**.

Bond	Bond energy/kJ mol^{-1}
H—H	436
O=O	498
O—H	464

....

....

....

....

.... [5]

6 The table below gives the enthalpies of combustion of four alcohols.

Alcohol	Molecular formula	Enthalpy of combustion/kJ mol^{-1}
Methanol	CH_3OH	−726
Ethanol	C_2H_5OH	−1370
Propan-1-ol	C_3H_7OH	−2010
Butan-1-ol	C_4H_9OH	−2670

a Plot a graph of the enthalpy of combustion against relative molecular mass for these four alcohols.

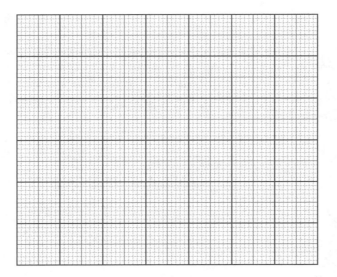

[4]

b i From your graph, predict the enthalpy change of combustion of pentan-1-ol.

.... [2]

    ii Explain how you obtained your answer to part **i**.

....

....

.... *[2]*

  c What can you say about the energy produced when alcohols of progressively higher molecular mass are burned in air?

.... *[1]*

7 In some countries, including Brazil, ethanol is mixed with petrol.

  a i Write a balanced chemical equation for the complete combustion of ethanol.

.... *[3]*

    ii Use the bond energy data in the tables below to calculate the enthalpy of combustion of ethanol.

Bond	Bond energy/kJ mol^{-1}
C—H	413
O=O	498
C=O	805

Bond	Bond energy/kJ mol^{-1}
H—O	464
C—C	347
C—O	358

....

....

....

....

.... *[5]*

  b In the manufacture of cars, an important factor that is considered is known as the *energy density*. This is the amount of energy released when 1 kg of the fuel is burned. It can be used to compare the energy efficiencies of different fuels. Using your answer to part **a ii**, and given that the enthalpy of combustion of hydrogen gas is -286 kJ mol^{-1}, calculate the energy density of both hydrogen and ethanol in kJ kg^{-1}.

....

.... *[4]*

  c Compare the energy density of hydrogen with that of ethanol and give a reason for the difference.

....

....

.... *[3]*

8 The diagram below shows an electrochemical cell that is based on the *first ever* chemical cell.

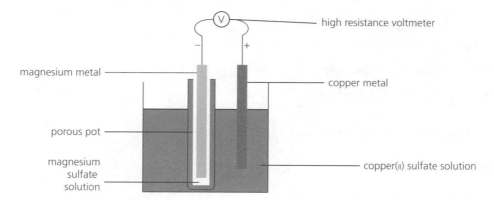

a The electrode reaction taking place at the anode is:

$Cu^{2+}(aq) + 2e^- \rightarrow Cu(s)$

Does this equation show oxidation or reduction? Explain your answer.

.... [2]

b Write an equation to show what occurs at the cathode, including state symbols.

.... [4]

c Which way would the electrons flow in the wire – from copper to magnesium or from

magnesium to copper? .... [1]

d What carries the electric current through the solutions? .... [1]

e What is the purpose of the porous pot?

.... [1]

Exam focus

Extended

1 An experiment was carried out to determine the enthalpy of combustion of butan-1-ol. The apparatus used is shown on the right. The heat source was a spirit burner containing butan-1-ol.

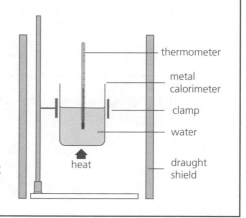

The mass of the spirit burner and butan-1-ol was recorded. It was allowed to burn for 4 minutes under a copper beaker that contained 500 cm³ of water. The initial temperature of the water was also recorded.

After 4 minutes, the mass of the spirit burner and the remaining butan-1-ol was recorded, as well as the final temperature of the water.

The results are shown below.

Initial mass of spirit burner and butan-1-ol = 29.42 g

Final mass of spirit burner and butan-1-ol = 27.51 g

Initial temperature of the water = 21.2 °C

Final temperature of the water = 42.0 °C

a   What mass of butan-1-ol was burned during the experiment? .... *[1]*

b   What was the temperature rise of the water during the experiment? .... *[1]*

c   Use the following relationship to find the energy transferred during the experiment in joules.
(The density of water is 1 g cm^{-3}.)

energy transferred = mass of water × 4.2 × temperature rise

....

.... *[3]*

d   How many moles of butan-1-ol were burned during the experiment? (A_r values: H = 1; C = 12; O = 16)

....

.... *[3]*

e   Using the results from this experiment, what is the enthalpy of combustion of butan-1-ol?

....

....

.... *[3]*

[Total: 11]

2   Hydrazine, H$_2$N—NH$_2$ has been used as a rocket fuel for many years. When it burns in oxygen gas, it reacts to form nitrogen gas and water as the only products.

a   Write a balanced chemical equation for the combustion of hydrazine.

.... *[3]*

b   When hydrazine undergoes combustion, a lot of energy is produced. Use the bond energies in the table to calculate the magnitude of this energy change.

Bond	Bond energy/kJ mol^{-1}
N—H	390
N—N	158
N≡N	946
O—H	464
O=O	498

....

....

.... *[5]*

c   If 240 kg of hydrazine was burned completely, what amount of heat energy would be released?
(A_r values: H = 1; N = 14)

....

.... *[3]*

[Total: 11]

7 Chemical reactions

● Core

1 a Chemical reactions occur faster at higher temperatures. Explain why this is the case.

....

.... [4]

b State four other factors that may affect the rate at which a chemical reaction occurs.

.... [4]

c Explain the meaning of each of the following terms.

   i activation energy

....

.... [2]

   ii successful collision

....

.... [2]

2 A student carried out a reaction between dilute hydrochloric acid and marble chips (calcium carbonate, $CaCO_3$) of different sizes. He placed a conical flask containing $50\,cm^3$ of hydrochloric acid solution onto a digital balance and then added 10 g of large marble chips. He inserted a piece of cotton wool into the neck of the flask. He recorded the loss in mass (in grams) against time.

He repeated the experiment but this time used 10 g of smaller marble chips.

His results are shown in the table below.

Time/min		0	½	1	1½	2	2½	3	3½	4	4½	5	5½	6	6½
Loss in mass/g	10 g of large marble chips	0	0.22	0.41	0.59	0.78	0.93	1.07	1.14	1.23	1.28	1.35	1.40	1.44	1.47
	10 g of small marble chips	0	0.45	0.82	1.15	1.35	1.50	1.61	1.66	1.68	1.69	1.70	1.70	1.70	1.70

a Write a balanced chemical equation for the reaction between the marble chips and hydrochloric acid.

.... [3]

b What was the purpose of the cotton wool that the student placed into the neck of the flask?

.... [2]

c Why did the mass decrease?

.... [1]

d Plot a graph of the loss in mass (vertical axis) against time (horizontal axis). You will need to draw two lines on the same axes, one for the small chips and one for the large chips.

[6]

e Which of the reactions was the fastest? How can you tell this from the graph?

.... [2]

● Core/Extended

3 The graphs on the right were produced by carrying out reactions between sulfuric acid and 2 g of magnesium in five different experiments.

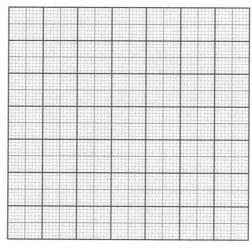

The experiments carried out involved:

I 2 g of magnesium ribbon and 40 cm³ of 0.1 mol dm⁻³ sulfuric acid at 25 °C

II 2 g of magnesium ribbon and 40 cm³ of 0.05 mol dm⁻³ sulfuric acid at 25 °C

III 2 g of magnesium powder and 40 cm³ of 0.1 mol dm⁻³ sulfuric acid at 25 °C

IV 2 g of magnesium powder and 20 cm³ of 0.1 mol dm⁻³ sulfuric acid at 25 °C

V 2 g of magnesium powder and 20 cm³ of 0.1 mol dm⁻³ sulfuric acid at 50 °C.

a Which of the two reactants is in excess?

.... [2]

b In the table below, write in the number of the experiment that is represented by each of the lines on the graph.

Line	A	B	C	D	E
Experiment					

[5]

c Explain why the reaction shown by line **B** occurs more rapidly than the reaction shown by line **C**.

.... *[2]*

d Explain why the reaction shown by line **D** occurs more rapidly than the reaction shown by line **E**.

.... *[2]*

● Extended

4 Explain each of the following using the collision theory.

a Reactions in solution occur faster if the solution has a high concentration.

....

.... *[3]*

b Powdered zinc metal reacts faster with hydrochloric acid to give hydrogen gas than strips of zinc metal do.

....

.... *[3]*

c A catalyst increases the rate of a chemical reaction.

....

.... *[3]*

5 A student carried out a reaction between sodium and water. The results she obtained are shown in the table below.

Time/s	0	10	20	30	40	50	60	70	80
Volume of H_2(g)/cm³	0	13	25	36	45	48	50	50	50

a Plot a graph of the volume of hydrogen produced (vertical axis) against time (horizontal axis).

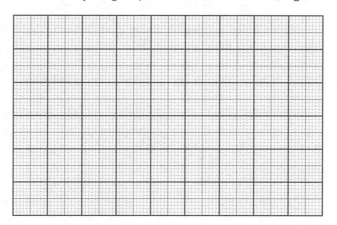

[4]

b i   When was the reaction the fastest? .... [1]

   ii How can you tell this from the graph?

   .... [1]

c Write a balanced chemical equation for the reaction between sodium and water.

   .... [3]

d What mass of sodium did the student use in the experiment?

   ....

   ....

   .... [3]

e How much hydrogen was produced in the experiment after:

   i   25 seconds? ....   [1]   ii 65 seconds? ....   [1]

f Which other Group I metal could the student have used, instead of sodium, to give a slower

   reaction with water? .... [1]

6 Cars are now fitted with catalytic converters to prevent carbon monoxide and nitrogen monoxide
   gases from passing into the atmosphere with the exhaust gases. The catalyst speeds up the reaction
   between carbon monoxide and nitrogen monoxide to produce carbon dioxide and nitrogen.

   a Write a balanced chemical equation for the reaction between carbon monoxide and nitrogen
      monoxide gases.

      .... [3]

   b The reaction you have written in part **a** shows both oxidation and reduction. Which of the
      reactants has been:

      i   oxidised? .... [1]   ii reduced? .... [1]

   c What catalyst is used in the catalytic converter?

      .... [1]

   d $5\,dm^3$ of petrol is combusted in a car engine. Assume that it is octane (C_8H_{18}), which has a density
      of $0.70\,g\,cm^{-3}$.

      i   Write a balanced chemical equation for the combustion of octane.

          .... [3]

      ii Calculate the mass of carbon dioxide that would be produced.

          ....

          ....

          .... [3]

iii What would be the total volume of carbon dioxide gas that would be produced?

.... *[2]*

iv If the car produced 100 g of carbon monoxide, what mass of carbon dioxide would this be converted to in the catalytic converter?

....

.... *[3]*

7 A student was trying to find out which of two transition metal oxides would be the best catalyst to decompose hydrogen peroxide (H_2O_2). Hydrogen peroxide is a colourless solution that decomposes to give water and oxygen gas.

a What is a catalyst?

....

.... *[2]*

b Write a balanced chemical equation for the decomposition of hydrogen peroxide.

.... *[3]*

c The table below shows the student's results.

Time/s		0	30	60	90	120	150	180	210	240
Volume of oxygen gas collected/cm³	5 g of manganese(IV) oxide	0	9	17	23	26	28	29	30	30
	5 g of copper(II) oxide	0	3	5	7	9	11	13	15	17

Plot a graph of the volume of oxygen produced (vertical axis) against time (horizontal axis). You will need to draw two lines on the same axes.

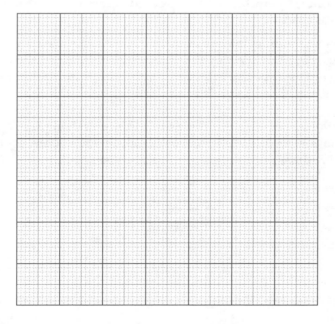

[6]

d Which of the two catalysts is the best? Explain your answer.

.... *[2]*

e Draw apparatus that could be used to carry out this experiment.

[4]

f What mass of copper(II) oxide would be obtained at the end of the experiment? Explain your answer.

....

.... [3]

Exam focus

Extended

1 This question is about a series of experiments involving the reaction between sodium thiosulfate and dilute hydrochloric acid.

$$Na_2S_2O_3(aq) + 2HCl(aq) \rightarrow 2NaCl(aq) + H_2O(l) + SO_2(g) + S(s)$$

The same amount of dilute hydrochloric acid was used in each experiment but the concentration of sodium thiosulfate was changed.

The volumes of water and sodium thiosulfate shown in the table below were put into a conical flask, which was placed on a pencil cross on a piece of paper. The acid was added and a stopwatch started. The student carrying out the experiment looked down through the flask at the cross and stopped the stopwatch when she could no longer see it.

Experiment	Volume of 0.2 mol dm⁻³ sodium thiosulfate/cm³	Volume of water/cm³	Concentration of sodium thiosulfate/ mol dm⁻³	Time for cross to become invisible/s	Rate of reaction/s⁻¹
1	100	0	0.2	25	4.0×10^{-2}
2	80	20	0.16	43	
3	60	40	0.12	65	
4	40	60	0.08	102	
5	20	80	0.04	160	

a Why was it important to keep the total volume of solution used in each experiment the same?

....

.... [2]

b Why did it become more difficult to see the cross on the paper as the reaction proceeded?

....

.... [2]

c Complete the table by calculating and writing in the rate of reaction for each of
   experiments **2** to **5**. [4]

d Plot a graph of the rate of reaction (vertical axis) against concentration of sodium thiosulfate
   (horizontal axis).

[4]

e Use your graph to find:

   i   the concentration of sodium thiosulfate at which the cross would become invisible after

       50 seconds. .... [1]

   ii the volume of sodium thiosulfate for which the cross would become invisible after 90 seconds.

       .... [1]

   iii the time you would expect the experiment to take if the concentration of sodium thiosulfate

       in the conical flask was $0.10\,mol\,dm^{-3}$. .... [1]

       [Total: 15]

2 A student carried out a series of reactions between zinc metal and dilute sulfuric acid. In each of the reactions he used the same mass of zinc (an excess) and the same volume of sulfuric acid. The graph below shows his results.

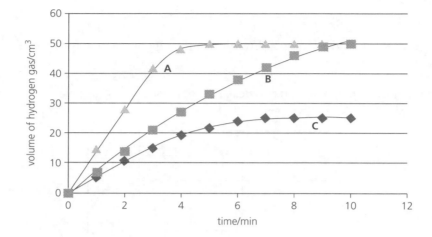

a Which was the fastest reaction? Explain how you can tell this from the graph.

.... [2]

b Which of the reactions was carried out:

   i   at the highest temperature? .... [1]

   ii using sulfuric acid of half the concentration used in the other two? .... [1]

c How could the rate of reaction **A** have been increased?

.... [1]

d What volume of 0.05 mol dm⁻³ sulfuric acid was used for reaction **C**?

....

....

.... [3]

e What was the total mass of hydrogen gas produced in reaction **A**?

....

.... [2]

[Total: 10]

8 Acids, bases and salts

● Core

1 Write word and balanced chemical equations for the reactions between each of the following pairs of substances.

   a   sodium carbonate and nitric acid

   ....

   .... [4]

   b   magnesium and hydrochloric acid

   ....

   .... [4]

2 Complete the table below, which is about the different methods of preparing soluble and insoluble salts.

Substances used to make the salt		Salt prepared	Other products
Calcium oxide	Hydrochloric acid		
	Sulfuric acid	Sodium sulfate	Water
Potassium carbonate		Potassium nitrate	Water and carbon dioxide
	Hydrochloric acid	Zinc chloride	Hydrogen
Lead nitrate	Sodium chloride		Sodium nitrate
Barium chloride	Potassium sulfate		

[8]

3 Explain how you would identify the presence, in solution, of each of the following ions.

   a   chloride, bromide and iodide ions

   i Cl^- .... [2]

   ii Br^- .... [2]

   iii I^- .... [2]

   b   carbonate ions .... [2]

   c   sulfate ions .... [2]

   d   iron(ii) and iron(iii) ions

   i Fe^{2+} .... [2]

   ii Fe^{3+} .... [2]

● Core/Extended

4   The diagram below shows some reactions of iron. Name and give the formulae of the substances **P** to **T** shown in the diagram.

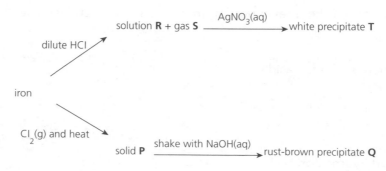

a   solid **P** .... *[2]*

b   rust-brown precipitate **Q** .... *[2]*

c   solution **R** .... *[2]*

d   gas **S** .... *[2]*

e   white precipitate **T** .... *[2]*

5   a   Use lines to link together the substance in Column A with its pH in Column B.

Column A	Column B
$0.1\,mol\,dm^{-3}$ HCl	13.0
$0.1\,mol\,dm^{-3}$ NaOH	7.0
$0.1\,mol\,dm^{-3}$ CH_3COOH	1.0
Pure H_2O	11.0
$0.1\,mol\,dm^{-3}$ NH_3 solution	2.9

[5]

b   Why are the pHs of $0.1\,mol\,dm^{-3}$ HCl and $0.1\,mol\,dm^{-3}$ CH_3COOH not the same?

....

....   *[3]*

● Extended

6   a   Write down the names of two chemical solutions that could be added together to form each of the following insoluble salts by a precipitation reaction.

i   silver chloride .... *[2]*

ii   barium sulfate .... *[2]*

iii   calcium carbonate .... *[2]*

b Give full experimental details to explain how you could prepare a sample of the yellow insoluble salt lead(II) iodide. In your account, you should name the reactants and give a balanced *ionic* equation, with state symbols, for the reaction you would carry out.

....

....

.... *[8]*

7 a What is the characteristic feature of an acid?

.... *[2]*

b Describe what is meant by each of the following terms.

i a weak acid .... *[2]*

ii a strong acid .... *[2]*

c Write equations to show:

i the ionisation of hydrochloric acid

.... *[2]*

ii the ionisation of ethanoic acid.

.... *[2]*

d Explain the difference between the terms *strong* and *weak acids* compared with *concentrated* and *dilute acids*.

....

.... *[4]*

Exam focus

Core/Extended

1 a Complete the following paragraph.

Acids dissolve in water to produce .... ions, which can be written as

.... Alkalis are soluble .... They dissolve in water to produce

.... ions, which can be written as .... Acids and alkalis react

together to produce solutions with a pH of 7; these are called .... reactions. *[6]*

b Write an ionic equation for the neutralisation reaction that takes place when an acid reacts with an alkali.

.... *[3]*

c In a reaction between potassium carbonate and hydrochloric acid to produce potassium chloride crystals, the following method was used.

25 cm^3 of hydrochloric acid was placed in a beaker. Solid potassium carbonate was added to the acid and effervescence was seen. The mixture was stirred and potassium carbonate was added until some remained at the bottom of the beaker. The mixture was then filtered and the filtrate collected in an evaporating basin. The filtrate was heated until about one half had evaporated and crystals were starting to form. The solution that remained was allowed to cool, and crystals formed.

i Write a balanced chemical equation for the reaction.

.... *[3]*

ii Why was potassium carbonate added until some remained at the bottom of the beaker?

.... *[1]*

iii What was the name of the filtrate? .... *[1]*

iv What name is given to a solution that has crystals starting to form from it?

.... *[1]*

[Total: 15]

Extended

2 a A reaction is carried out to prepare a sample of sodium sulfate crystals, starting from dilute sodium hydroxide and dilute sulfuric acid. The reaction is carried out using a titration. Explain clearly how you would prepare the sodium sulfate crystals.

....

....

....

....

.... *[7]*

b Write a balanced chemical equation for the reaction between sodium hydroxide and sulfuric acid.

.... *[3]*

[Total: 10]

9 The Periodic Table

● Core

1   There are five elements in Group VII of the Periodic Table. They are known as the halogens. The table below gives the melting and boiling points of the halogens. However, one of the values is missing.

Element	Atomic number	Melting point/K	Boiling point/K
F	9	54	85
Cl	17	172	239
Br	35	266	
I	53	387	458
At	85	576	610

a   Plot a graph of the melting and boiling points of the halogens against their atomic numbers. Join the plotted points for the melting points together and, in a different colour, the plotted points for the boiling points.

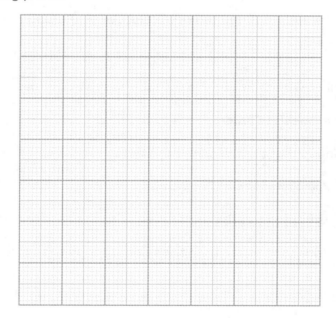

[6]

b   Use your graph to estimate the boiling point of bromine. ....   [1]

c   What is the trend in the melting points of the halogens?

....   [1]

d   Which of the halogens would be a gas at room temperature (298 K)?

....   [2]

2   Chlorine gas will react with aluminium metal using the apparatus shown below.

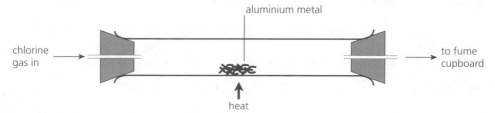

a   Write word and balanced symbol equations for the reaction between aluminium metal and chlorine gas.

....

.... [4]

b   Why is it necessary to ensure that the unreacted chlorine gas is passed into a fume cupboard?

.... [1]

c   Name a halogen that would react with aluminium metal more quickly than chlorine does.

.... [1]

d   Name a metal that would react with chlorine gas more quickly than aluminium does.

.... [1]

3   Complete the following passage.

The modern Periodic Table has been credited to the work of the Russian chemist

.... After many years of chemists across the world trying to classify

the elements in a useful way, he came up with the table that we have been using for nearly 150

years. He arranged the elements in order of increasing .... Occasionally he had

to swap elements around so that they were in the same .... as other elements with

similar properties, for example tellurium (Te) and .... (................). The major change that

he introduced to his classification was that he left .... for elements that had not been

discovered at the time. Today, the elements in the modern Periodic Table are arranged in order of

increasing ....   [7]

● Core/Extended

4   Element **Y** has a proton number of 19 and a relative atomic mass of 39.

a   i   How many electrons, protons and neutrons are there in an atom of element **Y**?

.... [3]

ii   What is the electronic configuration of this element? .... [1]

iii   In which group of the Periodic Table would you find this element? Explain your answer.

.... [2]

iv   What would be the symbol for the ion that element **Y** forms? .... [1]

b   The proton number of bromine (Br) is 35. It is in Group VII of the Periodic Table – it is a halogen.
   How many electrons will bromine have in its outer energy level? .... *[1]*

c   When potassium metal is heated and lowered into a gas jar of bromine vapour, a chemical
   reaction occurs, which produces white fumes.

   i   What do the white fumes consist of? .... *[1]*

   ii   Write word and balanced chemical equations for the reaction.

   ....

   .... *[4]*

   iii   When potassium is reacted with chlorine gas, the reaction is more vigorous. Explain this
        observation in terms of the reactivity of the halogens.

   ....

   ....

   .... *[3]*

5   The diagram below shows part of the Periodic Table.

Using the elements shown above, write down the symbol for an element that:

a   is a transition element .... *[1]*   e   has a full outer electron energy

b   has four electrons in its outer energy   level .... *[1]*

   level .... *[1]*   f   has an electronic configuration

c   is a liquid at room temperature and   of 2,8,5 .... *[1]*

   pressure .... *[1]*   g   is a Group I metal .... *[1]*

d   is stored under oil .... *[1]*   h   is a gaseous Group VII element. .... *[1]*

6   In 1817, Johann Döbereiner tried to organise the elements that were known at that time into an
   order that would be useful to other chemists. He put elements into groups of three called 'triads'.
   One of these groups contained the elements lithium, sodium and potassium.

   a   Describe how the reactions of these elements with water are:

   i   similar

   ....

   ....

   .... *[4]*

ii different.

....

.... [2]

Explain your answers in terms of the electronic structure and/or size of the atoms of the elements.

b In another group Döbereiner placed the elements strontium, barium and calcium.

i   In which group of the modern Periodic Table will you find these elements? .... [1]

ii How many electrons will each of these elements have in its outer energy level? .... [1]

iii Which of these elements will undergo the most vigorous reaction when added to water? Explain your answer in terms of its electronic structure.

....

.... [3]

7 This question is about the transition elements.

a Give two physical properties of transition elements that make them more useful to us than the Group I metals.

.... [2]

b i What type of chemical bonding is present in all transition elements? .... [1]

ii Draw a labelled diagram to show the type of chemical bonding present in transition elements.

[3]

c The transition elements, and their compounds, often make very good catalysts and are used extensively in industrial processes.

i   Explain why a catalyst would be used in an industrial process.

.... [2]

ii Give two examples of processes that use a transition element catalyst, or a compound of a transition element, and state the catalyst used.

....

.... [4]

Extended

8 Use the information given in the table below to answer the following questions about elements **A**, **B**, **C**, **D** and **E**.

Element	Proton number	Nucleon number	Electronic structure
A	10	20	2,8
B	19	39	2,8,8,1
C	13	27	
D	8	16	
E		35	2,8,7

a Complete the table by writing in:

  i   the electronic structure of elements **C** and **D**   [2]

  ii the proton number of element **E**.   [1]

b i   Which of these elements, **A** to **E**, is a noble gas? ....   [1]

  ii Which of these elements, **A** to **E**, is a Group I element? ....   [1]

  iii Which of these elements, **A** to **E**, is a Group VII element? ....   [1]

  iv Which of these elements, **A** to **E**, is aluminium? ....   [1]

c i   Which of these elements, **A** to **E**, will form an ion with a +3 charge? ....   [1]

  ii Which of these elements, **A** to **E**, will form an ion with a −2 charge? ....   [1]

  iii Which of these elements, **A** to **E**, will not form an ion? ....   [1]

Exam focus

Core

1 Displacement reactions occur when a solution containing a halide ion reacts with a more reactive halogen. This type of reaction can be seen when a solution of potassium bromide reacts with chlorine.

  a Write word and balanced chemical equations for the reaction that occurs between potassium bromide solution and chlorine.

  ....

  .... [3]

b Why is chlorine more reactive than bromine?

....

.... *[2]*

c Which other halogen would react with potassium bromide? .... *[1]*

d Would there be a reaction between a solution of sodium fluoride and bromine?
Explain your answer

.... *[2]*

[Total: 8]

Core/Extended

2 In the Periodic Table, elements are arranged in vertical columns called groups. Within each group, the elements have similar chemical reactions but show a trend in their physical properties such as reactivity and melting point.

a Consider the two elements potassium and sodium, both found in Group I of the Periodic Table.

i Give the electronic configurations of the elements sodium and potassium.

.... *[2]*

ii Which of these elements, potassium or sodium, is the more reactive when added to water? Explain your answer in terms of their atomic structure.

....

.... *[2]*

iii Write a balanced chemical equation for the reaction of sodium with water.

.... *[3]*

b In Group VII there are five elements, all of which have the same number of electrons in their outer energy level.

i How many electrons do these elements have in their outer energy level? .... *[1]*

ii What do all of these elements do when they react and form ions?

.... *[1]*

iii What would be the charge on an ion of any of the Group VII ions? .... *[1]*

iv Which of the Group VII elements would be the most reactive? Explain your answer.

....

.... *[3]*

[Total: 13]

(10) Metals

● Core

1 This question concerns the extraction of iron from its ore haematite (Fe_2O_3) in the blast furnace.

   a The coke that is added to the furnace fulfils two functions. What are they?

   ....

   .... [2]

   b Why is limestone added as a raw material to the furnace?

   .... [1]

   c Write chemical equations for each of the following processes, which occur in the blast furnace.

      i the thermal decomposition of limestone

      .... [3]

      ii the oxidation of carbon (coke)

      .... [3]

      iii the formation of carbon monoxide

      .... [3]

      iv the extraction of iron from the haematite

      .... [3]

      v the formation of calcium silicate (slag)

      .... [3]

   d What role does the carbon monoxide play in the extraction process? .... [1]

2 The table below gives the compositions and properties of some different types of steel and cast iron.

Type of steel	Composition	Properties
Cast iron	96% Fe, 4% C	Very brittle, easily moulded, hard
Mild steel	99.5% Fe, 0.5% C	Easily worked, little brittleness, springy
Hard steel	99% Fe, 1% C	Tougher than mild steel, brittle
Stainless steel	74% Fe, 18% Cr, 8% Ni	Tough, does not rust
Tungsten steel	95% Fe, 5% W	Tough even at high temperatures

   a i Which element that is present in steels and cast iron makes them brittle?

      .... [1]

      ii How is the amount of the element you have named in your answer to part i reduced during
         the steel-making process?

      .... [2]

b Stainless steel is a mixture of three different metals. What name do we give to substances such as stainless steel? .... [1]

c Cars and ships made from steel often suffer from rusting. Stainless steel, however, does not rust. Why do we not make cars or ships out of stainless steel?

.... [2]

d Complete the table below to give the properties required for the objects listed and the type of steel you would *choose* to make them out of.

Object	Properties	Steel
Chisel	Tough	Hard steel
Car body		
Axe		
Surgical knife		

[6]

3 A student set up the experiment below to find out what conditions were needed for rusting to occur.

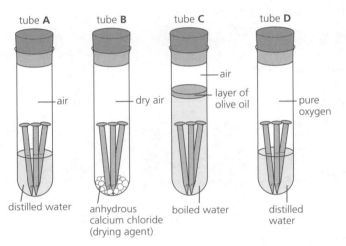

a What was the purpose of:

   i the anhydrous calcium chloride in tube **B**?

   .... [2]

   ii boiling the water in tube **C**?

   .... [2]

   iii the layer of oil in tube **C**?

   .... [2]

b What conditions were present in each of the tubes? Put ticks in the table below to show if oxygen or water were present in each of the tubes.

Tube	Water	Oxygen
A		
B		
C		
D		

[4]

c i   In which tube(s) will the nails not rust? .... [2]

   ii Explain your answer to part **i**.

      .... [2]

d i   In which tube will the nails rust the most? .... [1]

   ii Explain your answer to part **i**.

      .... [1]

● Core/Extended

4 Complete and balance the following chemical equations.

a .... + H_2SO_4(aq) → $MgSO_4$(aq) + H_2O(l) + ... [2]

b $2Ca$(s) + O_2(g) → .... [1]

c Mg(s) + ... → $MgSO_4$(aq) + Zn(s) [1]

d .... + ... → $2MgO$(s) [2]

e Zn(s) + 2 .... (aq) → .... + H_2(g) [2]

● Extended

5 The list below shows four metals in order of their chemical reactivity. Use it to answer the questions that follow.

| (most reactive) zinc iron tin copper (least reactive) |

a i   Write a balanced symbol equation for the reaction that occurs when zinc powder (grey) is added to copper(II) sulfate solution (blue).

      .... [3]

   ii What changes would you see when the zinc is added to copper(II) sulfate solution?

      .... [2]

   iii Explain what happens to cause the changes you have described in your answer to part **ii**.

      .... [2]

b Iron cans for storing food are usually coated with a layer of tin. Give two reasons why tin is a suitable metal for this purpose.

   .... [2]

6 Write balanced chemical equations for the reactions between each of the following pairs of substances.

a lithium metal and water

.... [3]

b zinc metal and hydrochloric acid

.... [3]

c magnesium and copper(ɪɪ) oxide

.... [3]

d lead and silver nitrate solution

.... [3]

e zinc metal and steam

.... [3]

f magnesium metal and water

.... [3]

7 A student carried out an experiment to find the order of reactivity of six different metals, labelled **A** to **F**. Small strips of each metal were placed into solutions of the nitrates of the other five metals. The student looked for a reaction occurring in each case.

a What would the student be looking for to see if a reaction was occurring?

.... [1]

b If a reaction did occur, what type of reaction would the student be observing?

.... [1]

c The table below shows a record of the student's results.

Metal	A nitrate	B nitrate	C nitrate	D nitrate	E nitrate	F nitrate
A	—	✓	✗	✗	✓	✓
B	✗	—	✗	✗	✓	✓
C	✓	✓	—	✓	✓	✓
D	✓	✓	✗	—	✓	✓
E	✗	✗	✗	✗	—	✗
F	✗	✗	✗	✗	✓	—

✓ reaction occurred   ✗ no reaction   — reaction not done

Put the metals **A** to **F** in order of their reactivity, with the least reactive metal first.

.... [3]

8 When a mixture of copper(II) oxide and zinc metal reacts, a pink-brown solid is formed along with a yellow solid that changes colour to white when it gets cold.

a Write word and balanced chemical equations for the reaction that occurs.

....

.... *[3]*

b Name the pink-brown solid that is formed in the reaction. .... *[1]*

c Name the solid that is yellow when hot and white when cold. .... *[1]*

d i Which of the reactants is being oxidised in this reaction? .... *[1]*

ii Explain why this reactant is being oxidised.

.... *[1]*

iii What is happening to the other reactant when the reaction occurs?

.... *[1]*

Exam focus

Core/Extended

1 Look at the flow diagram shown below.

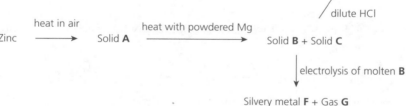

a Name and give the formulae of substances **A** to **I**.

A .... *[1]*   F .... *[1]*

B .... *[1]*   G .... *[1]*

C .... *[1]*   H .... *[1]*

D .... *[1]*   I .... *[1]*

E .... *[1]*

b Write balanced chemical equations for the reactions in which:

i solid **B** was formed

.... *[2]*

ii solution **D** and gas **E** were formed.

.... *[3]*

c Write anode and cathode reactions for the processes that take place during the electrolysis of molten **B**.

....

.... *[6]*

[Total: 20]

2 Use the reactivity series on the right to answer the questions that follow.

a When lead(II) oxide reacts with iron, a redox reaction occurs.

   i Write a balanced chemical equation for the reaction.

.... *[2]*

   ii What is a *redox reaction*?

.... *[2]*

   iii Describe what is happening to the iron and the lead(II) oxide when the reaction occurs.

.... *[2]*

sodium
magnesium
zinc
iron
lead
hydrogen
copper
silver

increasing reactivity

b Magnesium reacts with hydrochloric acid to give a salt and hydrogen gas.

   i Write a balanced chemical equation for the reaction.

.... *[3]*

   ii Copper metal does not react with acid. Explain why the reaction does not occur for copper but does occur for magnesium.

.... *[2]*

   iii Name another metal that will not react with hydrochloric acid. .... *[1]*

c Zinc oxide is unusual in that it changes colour when it is heated. It is yellow when hot but white when cold. When zinc oxide reacts with magnesium metal, a white solid is obtained 10 minutes after the reaction has ended.

   i What is the white solid? .... *[1]*

   ii Write a balanced chemical equation for the reaction.

.... *[2]*

   iii What would happen to the white solid obtained if it were heated?

.... *[1]*

[Total: 16]

11 Air and water

● Core

1 Helium, neon and argon are noble gases found in the atmosphere.

    a Which group in the Periodic Table do these elements belong to? .... [1]

    b The atomic numbers and mass numbers of these elements are given below.

$$^{4}_{2}He \qquad ^{20}_{10}Ne \qquad ^{40}_{18}Ar$$

        i What are the electronic structures of each of these elements?

        ....

        ....

        .... [3]

        ii Why are these elements classified as inert gases?

        .... [1]

        iii When elements combine by means of covalent bonds, what electronic structure do they try to achieve in their outer electron energy level?

        .... [2]

    c Give a use for each of these gases based on their inert nature.

    ....

    ....

    .... [3]

2 Water pollution has become a real problem. Water is such a good solvent that many substances will dissolve in it, including fertilisers.

    a Explain how fertilisers get into rivers.

    ....

    .... [2]

    b Give the names and formulae of the nitrogen-containing ions, from chemical fertilisers, that pollute water in rivers.

    .... [4]

    c Name and give the formula of an artificial fertiliser that contains the ions you have named in your answer to part **b**.

    .... [2]

d i What organisms are encouraged to grow in rivers by the presence of artificial fertilisers?

.... [2]

ii What effect does the growth of these organisms have on life in the river?

....

.... [2]

3 As well as the substances you would expect in pure dry air, other substances called pollutants are found in the atmosphere. These pollutants cause air pollution.

a Explain the meaning of the two sentences above, using specific examples where possible.

....

....

.... [3]

b Sulfur dioxide is a pollutant. Major sources of this gas are heavy industry and power stations.

i From which three substances would sulfur dioxide be produced in these industries?

.... [3]

ii The word and balanced chemical equations for the production of sulfur dioxide are given below.

sulfur + oxygen → sulfur dioxide

$S(s) + O_2(g) → SO_2(g)$

Calculate the mass of sulfur dioxide produced by 32 kg of sulfur. (A_r values: O = 16; S = 32)

.... [1]

iii The sulfur dioxide dissolves in water in the atmosphere and produces an acid. This acid is then oxidised to give a different acid. What are the names and formulae of the initial acid and the final acid produced on oxidation?

.... [4]

iv What problems do the acids produced from sulfur dioxide in the air cause in the environment?

....

....

.... [3]

v Units are being added to some power stations to prevent the emission of sulfur dioxide. What is the name given to these units?

.... [1]

● Core/Extended

4 Nitrogen gas was discovered by Daniel Rutherford in 1772. It is now known to be a very important gas in the atmosphere. It is also an element that is essential for the well-being of animals and plants.

a It is known that nitrogen atoms have an atomic number of 7. What information does this give you about atoms of nitrogen?

....

....

.... *[4]*

b Nitrogen is a *diatomic gas and contains a triple bond between the nitrogen atoms.* With the aid of a bonding diagram, showing the outermost energy levels only, show that you understand the meaning of the phrase in italics.

....

.... *[5]*

c i Which of the bonds found in oxygen and nitrogen molecules is the strongest?

.... *[1]*

ii Explain your answer to part **i**.

....

.... *[3]*

d Give two uses for nitrogen.

.... *[2]*

5 a Nitrogen is one of the three essential mineral elements needed by plants.

i What type of compound in plants, essential for their growth, contains nitrogen?

.... *[1]*

ii What are the other two essential mineral elements needed by plants for healthy growth?

.... *[2]*

b The nitrogen needed by plants can be obtained by two different routes. Some plants are able to take nitrogen directly from the air whilst others obtain their nitrogen from the soil.

i Name a plant that is able to take nitrogen directly from the air. .... *[1]*

ii How do farmers ensure that there is sufficient nitrogen in the soil for their crops to

grow healthily?.. *[1]*

c Calculate the percentage of nitrogen in each of these nitrogen compounds used by farmers.

    i   sodium nitrate, $NaNO_3$

....

[1]

    ii   ammonium phosphate, $(NH_4)_3PO_4$

....

[1]

    iii   urea, $CO(NH_2)_2$

....

[1]

    iv   ammonium sulfate, $(NH_4)_2SO_4$

....

[1]

● Extended

6 Oxides of nitrogen are atmospheric pollutants. Motor vehicles are responsible for much of the pollution by these oxides that is found in the atmosphere in towns and cities.

    a Nitrogen monoxide is formed by the reaction of nitrogen and oxygen inside the car engine. The word and symbol equations are given below.

       nitrogen + oxygen → nitrogen monoxide

       $N_2(g) + O_2(g) \rightarrow 2NO(g)$

       i   Calculate the volume of nitrogen monoxide produced at room temperature from $48\,dm^3$ of nitrogen.

       ....

[1]

       ii   As it exits the exhaust, the nitrogen monoxide produced in the car engine then reacts with oxygen from the air and forms the brown gas nitrogen(IV) oxide. This is an acidic gas. The word and symbol equations are given below.

          nitrogen monoxide + oxygen → nitrogen(IV) oxide

          $NO(g) + O_2(g) \rightarrow NO_2(g)$

          Balance the chemical equation above.

       .... [2]

iii What attachment to a car would help to eliminate the problem of pollution by oxides of

nitrogen? .... [1]

b When nitrogen(IV) oxide reacts with water from the atmosphere, an acid is produced along with some nitrogen monoxide.

i Name and give the formula of the acid produced.

.... [2]

ii Write word and balanced chemical equations for the production of this acid.

....

.... [4]

7 The gases in the air can be separated by fractional distillation of liquid air. In this process, water vapour and carbon dioxide are removed from the air. The remaining gases in the air are then liquefied and separated by fractional distillation. The table shows these gases, along with their boiling points.

Gas	Boiling point/°C
Argon	−186
Helium	−269
Krypton	−157
Neon	−246
Nitrogen	−196
Oxygen	−183
Xenon	−108

a How are solid particles removed from the air before the carbon dioxide and any water vapour are removed?

.... [1]

b To what temperature is the air cooled to remove the carbon dioxide and water vapour? .... [1]

c Before distilling the air, it is cooled to below −200°C at high pressure.

i Why is it necessary to remove the carbon dioxide and water vapour from the air before the temperature is taken down to −200°C?

....

.... [2]

ii Which of the gases will not become liquids at −200°C? .... [2]

iii Which two gases are difficult to separate by this method? .... [2]

iv Explain your answer to part **iii**.

.... [1]

d Explain how the liquid air is separated by fractional distillation.

....

....

....

.... [4]

Exam focus

Core

1   Water is very good at dissolving substances. It is, therefore, very unusual to find really pure water on this planet. The questions that follow are about the purification of water from a reservoir.

a   i   How is filtration of the water from the reservoir carried out?

.... [1]

ii   What is the purpose of filtering at this stage?

.... [1]

b   Chlorine is added to the water near the end of the purification process. Why is chlorine added?

.... [1]

c   Chlorine produces an acidic solution containing two acids. The incomplete chemical equation is shown below. The acid shown as a product is called chloric(I) acid.

$$Cl_2(g) + H_2O(l) \rightarrow \text{...................} (aq) + HOCl(aq)$$

What are the name and formula of the other acid that is produced?

.... [2]

d   Why is sodium hydroxide added after chlorination?

.... [1]

e   To prevent tooth decay, an ion is often added to the water before it is supplied to homes. Name

this ion and give its formula. .... [2]

f   i   Tap water usually contains some chloride ions rather than chlorine. Describe a chemical test that would show that tap water does contain chloride ions.

....

....

.... [3]

ii   Explain in terms of electronic configurations what happens to chlorine when it is converted into chloride ions.

....

....

.... [3]

[Total: 14]

Extended

2 Gaseous ammonia is manufactured in large quantities. The process by which it is manufactured was developed by Fritz Haber in 1911 and first used industrially in 1913. The production of this important chemical is affected both by the temperature and by the pressure at which the process is run. The equation that represents the synthesis of ammonia is:

$$N_2(g) + 3H_2(g) \rightarrow 2NH_3(g)$$

An iron catalyst is used.

The graph shows how the percentage yield of ammonia changes with temperature and pressure.

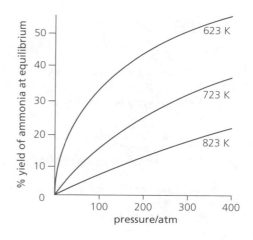

a Using the graph, state:

   i   the effect of increasing the pressure on the yield of ammonia

   .... [2]

   ii   the effect of decreasing the temperature on the yield of ammonia.

   .... [1]

b Explain why the change you have described in part **a i** occurs with increasing pressure.

   ....

   ....

   .... [3]

c Using your answer to part **a ii**, deduce the sign of the energy change that occurs during the production of ammonia. Explain your answer.

   ....

   ....

   .... [3]

d The conditions used in industry for the production of ammonia are a pressure of 200 atmospheres and a temperature of 723 K. What is the percentage yield of ammonia under these conditions? .... [1]

e Why is a temperature lower than 723 K not used?

   ....

   .... [2]

[Total: 12]

12 Sulfur

● Core

1 a Rainwater is naturally acidic.

   i Explain why this is the case.

   .... [2]

   ii What is the expected pH of naturally acidic rainwater? .... [1]

   iii Another acid is found in rain, which is caused by human activity producing oxides

   of nitrogen. Give the name and formula of this acid... [2]

 b In many parts of the world, the pH of rainwater has fallen.

   i What is the pH of the acid rain found in many parts of the world?

   .... [1]

   ii Give two problems associated with acid rain.

   .... [2]

● Core/Extended

2 For each of the following statements, write either 'true' or 'false'.

 a Sulfur is a metallic element. .... [1]

 b Sulfur reacts with burning magnesium to form magnesium sulfide. .... [1]

 c Initially when sulfur dioxide dissolves in rainwater it forms sulfurous acid. .... [1]

 d Concentrated sulfuric acid cannot remove the water of crystallisation from $CuSO_4.5H_2O$.

   .... [1]

 e In medicine, magnesium sulfate is used as a laxative. .... [1]

 f The formation of SO_3 in the Contact process is a reversible reaction. .... [1]

3 Draw lines to link each substance on the left with the correct description on the right.

a	$H_2S_2O_7$
b	$CaSO_4$
c	SO_2
d	$KHSO_4$
e	MAZIT metals
f	$BaSO_4$
g	Concentrated H_2SO_4

A	Formed when testing for a sulfate
B	A powerful dehydrating agent
C	Will react with dilute sulfuric acid
D	A main cause of acid rain
E	Used in making detergents
F	A normal salt of sulfuric acid
G	An acid salt

[7]

● Extended

4 The scheme below shows some reactions of dilute sulfuric acid.

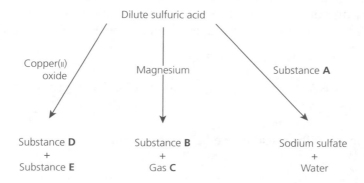

a Name and give the formulae of substances **A** to **E**.

A .... [2]

B .... [2]

C .... [2]

D .... [2]

E .... [2]

b Write word and balanced chemical equations for the reactions in which substance **A** reacts and substances **B**, **C**, **D** and **E** are formed.

....

....

....

....

....

.... [9]

c Describe a chemical test to confirm the identity of gas **C**.

....

.... [2]

5 The real acidity in acid rain is mainly caused by sulfuric acid. The amount of this acid can be determined by carrying out a titration. The results below came from a titration of a sample of acid rain with sodium hydroxide solution. The neutralisation reaction taking place is:

$H_2SO_4(aq) + 2NaOH(aq) \rightarrow Na_2SO_4(aq) + 2H_2O(l)$

25.00 cm³ of acid rain was just neutralised by 15.00 cm³ of a 0.10 mol dm⁻³ sodium hydroxide solution. Calculate:

a the concentration of sulfuric acid in the acid rain solution

....

.... [3]

b the amount of sulfuric acid in 1000 litres of acid rain.

....

.... [3]

c Acid rain (mainly sulfuric acid) attacks steel structures (mainly iron). Write word and balanced chemical equations for the reaction that takes place.

....

.... [3]

6 Car body parts are made from sheet steel. Before the car body parts are painted, the metal must be free from rust, Fe_2O_3. To ensure that the steel is rust free, the sheets are dipped into sulfuric acid. An unbalanced chemical equation for this process is:

$$Fe_2O_3(s) + H_2SO_4(aq) \rightarrow Fe_2(SO_4)_3(aq) + H_2O(l)$$

a Balance the chemical equation above.

.... [2]

b The steel sheets are only left in the acid for a short time. Why are they not left in for longer?

....

....

.... [3]

c Sulfuric acid is used in the manufacture of the fertiliser $(NH_4)_2SO_4$. What is the name of this

substance? .... [1]

d To make the fertiliser in part **c**, sulfuric acid has to be neutralised by an alkaline substance. In this case, a possible alkaline substance to use is ammonia solution, NH_4OH.

  i Explain what you understand by the term *neutralised* with respect to this reaction.

  ....

  ....

  .... [3]

  ii The balanced chemical equation for the reaction between ammonium hydroxide and sulfuric acid is:

  $$2NH_4OH(aq) + H_2SO_4(aq) \rightarrow (NH_4)_2SO_4(aq) + 2H_2O(l)$$

  Calculate the amount of ammonium sulfate fertiliser produced from 196 tonnes of sulfuric acid. (A_r values: H = 1; C = 12; N = 14; O = 16)

  ....

  ....

  ....

  .... [4]

Exam focus

Extended

1 When manufacturing sulfuric acid, sulfur dioxide is first made into sulfur trioxide.

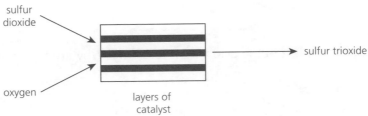

sulfur dioxide

oxygen

layers of catalyst

sulfur trioxide

a Give three reasons why a catalyst is used in this reaction.

   ....

   .... [3]

b Name and give the formula of the catalyst used in this process.

   .... [2]

c Write word and balanced chemical equations for the making of sulfur trioxide.

   ....

   .... [4]

d The reaction in part **c** goes almost to completion. What does this mean with respect to this reaction?

   ....

   .... [2]

e The sulfur trioxide produced is then dissolved in concentrated sulfuric acid.

   $SO_3(g) + H_2SO_4(l) \rightarrow H_2S_2O_7(l)$

   i   Give the name of the substance $H_2S_2O_7$. .... [1]

   ii Why is sulfur trioxide not dissolved directly into water to form concentrated sulfuric acid?

      ....

      .... [2]

f With the aid of a balanced chemical equation, explain how concentrated sulfuric acid is made from $H_2S_2O_7$.

   ....

   ....

   .... [4]

g   Give two uses for concentrated sulfuric acid.

.... *[2]*

[Total: 20]

2   It has been found in recent years that the sulfuric acid in acid rain reacts with limestone, which is eaten away by the following process.

$CaCO_3(s) + H_2SO_4(aq) \rightarrow CaSO_4(s) + H_2O(l) + CO_2(g)$

a   Write the ionic equation for the above reaction.

.... *[3]*

b   What other pollutant gases, apart from sulfur dioxide, contribute to acid rain?

.... *[1]*

c   i   How many moles of calcium carbonate are there in 150 g of calcium carbonate? (A_r values: C = 12; O = 16)

....

....

.... *[3]*

ii   Calculate the mass of carbon dioxide formed when 150 g of calcium carbonate reacts with excess sulfuric acid.

....

....

.... *[3]*

iii   The amount of sulfuric acid in rainwater has increased over the years. Explain the reasons for this.

....

....

.... *[3]*

[Total: 13]

● Core

1 Limestone is a very important raw material in a number of industries.

   a What do you understand by the term *raw material*?

   .... [2]

   b Give three important uses for limestone.

   ....

   .... [3]

   c Limestone is obtained by open-cast mining. What are the advantages and disadvantages to the local community of an open-cast limestone mine in their area?

   ....

   ....

   ....

   .... [6]

2 a i Calcium hydroxide, or slaked lime, is a cheap industrial alkali. Explain the meaning of the term *alkali*.

   ....

   .... [3]

   ii Give two large-scale uses for calcium hydroxide.

   .... [2]

   b i A weak solution of calcium hydroxide in water is called limewater. It is used to test for carbon dioxide gas. Explain what happens in this test, giving the chemical name and formula of the major substance produced during the test.

   ....

   .... [3]

   ii If carbon dioxide is passed through limewater continuously, a further change takes place. Describe what happens to the limewater solution and give an explanation of what is happening, along with the name and formula of the major product.

   ....

   .... [4]

   iii If calcium hydroxide is mixed with sand, what useful building material is produced?

   .... [1]

3   The diagram shows the limestone cycle.

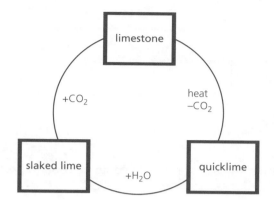

a   Give the chemical name and formula for:

   i   limestone .... [2]

   ii   quicklime .... [2]

   iii   slaked lime .... [2]

b   Slaked lime is sometimes used for *neutralising* soil acidity. One of the causes of soil acidity is *acid rain* and the sulfuric acid found in it in particular.

   i   What do you understand by the words and phrases in italics?

   ....

   ....

   ....

   .... [4]

   ii   Write a word and balanced chemical equation for the reaction that takes place when the acid in the soil is neutralised in this way.

   ....

   .... [4]

4   In recent years, scientists have detected an increase in the amount of carbon dioxide in the atmosphere. Carbon dioxide is a *greenhouse gas* and has been linked to *global warming*.

a   Explain the meaning of each of the following terms.

   i   greenhouse gas ....

   .... [2]

   ii   global warming ....

   .... [2]

b   Describe the effect that global warming will have on the Earth over time.

   ....

   ....   *[3]*

● Core/Extended

5   a   Draw a labelled diagram of the apparatus that could be used to prepare a sample of carbon dioxide.

   [6]

   b   If you wanted a dry sample of the gas, how would you alter the apparatus to allow you to obtain this dry sample? Name any chemical substances you would use.

   ....

   ....

   ....   *[4]*

   c   i   Carbon dioxide will only allow very strongly burning substances, such as magnesium, to continue burning in it. Describe what you would see during this reaction.

      ....

      ....

      ....   *[3]*

      ii   Balance the following chemical equation for this reaction.

      .... $Mg(s)$ + ... $CO_2(g) \rightarrow$ .... $MgO(s)$ + ... $C(s)$ *[2]*

      iii   Write the word equation for this reaction.

      ....   *[1]*

      iv   This is a redox reaction. What do you understand by the term *redox reaction*?

      ....   *[2]*

      v   Name and give the formulae of the reducing and oxidising agents in this reaction.

      ....

      ....   *[4]*

6 a Burning fossil fuels makes a large contribution to the amount of carbon dioxide in the atmosphere.

   i Coal is a fossil fuel. What is a *fossil fuel*?

   .... [2]

   ii Methane gas is also a fossil fuel. It usually occurs together with a further fossil fuel. Give the

   name of this other fossil fuel. .... [1]

   iii The balanced chemical equation for burning methane in air is:
   $CH_4(g) + 2O_2(g) \rightarrow CO_2(g) + 2H_2O(l)$

   Calculate the mass of carbon dioxide produced when 32 g of methane is burned.
   (A_r values: H = 1; C = 12; O = 16)

   ....

   .... [2]

   iv What volume of carbon dioxide would be produced when 32 g of methane is burned?
   (1 mole of gas occupies 24 dm³ at room temperature and pressure.)

   ....

   .... [2]

 b The formula of the major constituent of petrol is C_8H_{18}. Explain why you would expect petrol to
 produce more carbon dioxide than methane when it is burned inside car engines.

   .... [1]

Exam focus

Core

1 Marble is a naturally occurring form of calcium carbonate, $CaCO_3$. When marble is heated, it
  decomposes in a chemical reaction to form quicklime by an endothermic reaction.

   a i Give the chemical name and formula of substance **A**. .... [2]

     ii Give the name and formula of the further substance that is produced during the

        decomposition of marble... [2]

     iii What has to be added to substance **A** to make substance **B**? .... [1]

     iv Give the chemical name and formula of substance **B**.. [2]

b   Explain the term *endothermic reaction* as applied to the decomposition of marble.

....

.... *[2]*

c   Name a further naturally occurring form of calcium carbonate. .... *[1]*

d   Give one use for each of substances **A** and **B**.

....

.... *[2]*

[Total: 12]

Core/Extended

2   Limestone is a very important industrial substance. It can be converted into quicklime in a kiln. A simplified diagram of this is shown on the right.

a   How is the kiln heated?

.... *[1]*

b   Why do you think hot air is blown through the kiln?

....

.... *[2]*

c   The main reaction in the kiln involves the thermal decomposition of calcium carbonate. The balanced chemical equation is:

$CaCO_3(s) \rightarrow CaO(s) + CO_2(g)$

i   What do you understand by the term *thermal decomposition*?

....

.... *[2]*

ii   What mass of quicklime can be made from 100 tonnes of limestone?
    (A_r values: C = 12; O = 16; Ca = 40)

.... *[1]*

d   In addition to the above reaction in the kiln, there is a further reaction taking place in which carbon dioxide is produced. Write word and balanced chemical equations for this reaction.

....

.... *[4]*

e   Modern kilns have been converted to be heated with a gaseous fuel. Name and give the formula of a possible gaseous fuel that could be used safely in this process.

.... *[2]*

[Total: 12]

(14) Organic 1

● Core

1 *Cracking* using a *catalyst* is one of the most important chemical processes carried out by the oil industry. Cracking involves the *thermal decomposition* of the fractions containing the larger *alkane* molecules. The process produces a mixture of *saturated* and *unsaturated* molecules.

Explain the meaning of each of the following terms.

a cracking .... [2]

b catalyst .... [2]

c thermal decomposition .... [2]

d alkane .... [2]

e saturated .... [2]

f unsaturated .... [2]

2 a Use the words below to complete the following passage about plastics.

addition polymer, polymerisation, monomers, chains, polymers, macromolecules, ethene

When small molecules such as .... join together to form long ....

of atoms, called ...., the process is called .... The small molecules

like ethene that join together in this way are called .... The polymer formed with

ethene is an .... Polymers are often referred to as .... [7]

b Other addition polymers include PVC and PTFE. Give the chemical name of:

i PVC .... [1]

ii PTFE .... [1]

c Name and draw the monomer unit that each of these polymers is made from.

i PVC ....

[2]

ii PTFE ....

[2]

d Draw part of the polymer chain for each of these two addition polymers.

   i PVC

   [1]

   ii PTFE

   [1]

e Give two uses for:

   i PVC .... *[2]*

   ii PTFE. .... *[2]*

3 a Ethene, C_2H_4, is the starting material for making plastic carrier bags.

   i Name the type of chemical change taking place in the diagram above.

   .... *[1]*

   ii Name the product formed by this reaction. .... *[1]*

   iii The alkene ethene is made by cracking large alkane molecules. Describe a simple chemical test to show that ethene is present.

   .... *[2]*

 b The majority of carrier bags are difficult to dispose of.

   i Explain why carrier bags should not just be thrown away.

   ....
   ....
   .... *[4]*

   ii Explain why the majority of plastic carrier bags are recycled.

   ....
   .... *[2]*

   iii Give one advantage that a plastic carrier bag has over one made out of paper.

   .... *[1]*

● Core/Extended

4 a Alkanes are unreactive compounds. They are not affected by many substances. Name two common classes of substance that they do not react with.

.... [2]

b The most important property of alkanes is that they will generally burn quite easily. The gaseous alkanes are some of the most useful fuels. When a gas like methane burns in a plentiful supply of air, which type of combustion does it undergo?

.... [1]

c What is the common name for methane? .... [1]

d The balanced chemical equation for the burning of methane in a plentiful supply of air is given below.

$$CH_4(g) + 2O_2(g) \rightarrow CO_2(g) + 2H_2O(g) \qquad \Delta H = -ve$$

i What does the sign of ΔH tell you about the reaction?

.... [1]

ii How many moles of carbon dioxide are produced by 1 mole of methane? .... [1]

iii What mass of carbon dioxide would be produced by 64 g of methane burning in a plentiful supply of air? (A_r values: H = 1; C = 12; O = 16)

.... [2]

iv What volume of carbon dioxide would be produced when 100 dm³ of methane is burned in a plentiful supply of air? (1 mole of any gas occupies 24 dm³ at room temperature and pressure.)

....

.... [2]

● Extended

5 a What structural feature does an alkene possess that an alkane does not?

.... [1]

b The diagram on the right shows the outer energy levels of the elements present in the compound ethene. Complete the bonding diagram by drawing dots and crosses to show the electrons in the overlap areas.

[5]

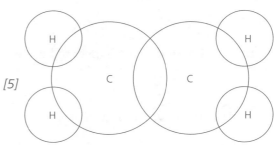

6 Give the name and structural formula of the main organic product(s) formed when each of the
   following chemical procedures is carried out.

   a A mixture of methane and chlorine is exposed to ultraviolet light. ....

                                                                                              [2]

   b A mixture of ethene and steam is passed over an acid catalyst at high temperature and pressure.

      ....

                                                                                              [2]

   c A mixture of ethene and hydrogen is passed over a metal catalyst at a high temperature.

      ....

                                                                                              [2]

   d Ethene is bubbled into a solution of bromine in 1,1,1-trichloroethane.

      ....

                                                                                              [2]

   e Decane is passed over a heated catalyst. ....

                                                                                              [4]

7 a Explain the meaning of the term *isomer* with reference to the molecule C_4H_{10}. Name and draw
      the structures of any substances you include in your answer.

      ....

      ....

                                                                                              [6]

   b i What would you expect to be the relative boiling points of the isomers you have drawn in part **a**?

         .... *[1]*

      ii Explain why the isomers you have drawn in part **a** have different boiling points.

          ....

          .... *[2]*

Exam focus

Core/Extended

1 The diagram shows the apparatus used in the cracking of a liquid alkane. Some of the labels have been replaced with letters.

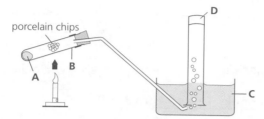

a For each letter, write down the correct label from the list below.

| gaseous alkene | hard glass boiling tube | paraffin-soaked mineral wool | water |

A .... *[1]*

B .... *[1]*

C .... *[1]*

D .... *[1]*

b What is the purpose of the porcelain chips in this experiment?

.... *[2]*

c Give an explanation of the following observation: 'The substance collected in the test-tube was found to decolourise bromine dissolved in an organic solvent.'

....

....

.... *[3]*

d Draw a star on the diagram above to show the position where you would introduce a further piece of apparatus to collect any liquid product. *[1]*

e An explosive element gas can also be produced in this process. Give the name and formula

of this gas. .... *[2]*

f i Complete the following symbol equation for a possible cracking of dodecane.

$C_{12}H_{26} \rightarrow C_4H_8 +$ .... *[1]*

ii Name the products of the reaction shown in the equation in part **i**.

.... *[2]*

[Total: 15]

Extended

2 a The alkanes form a homologous series of hydrocarbons obtained from crude oil. What do you understand by the terms *homologous series* and *hydrocarbons*?

....

....

.... [5]

b i The first four members of the alkane family are shown in the table below.

Alkane	Formula	Structure
Methane		H │ H — C — H │ H
Ethane	C_2H_6	
Propane		H H H │ │ │ H — C — C — C — H │ │ │ H H H
Butane		

Complete the table by filling in the missing formulae and structures. [5]

ii Name the type of bonding present in alkanes. .... [2]

iii By showing the outer electron energy levels, draw a diagram to show the chemical bonding in a molecule of ethane.

[4]

iv All the alkanes shown in the table above are gases. What would be the physical difference between these four alkanes and the alkane decane, $C_{10}H_{22}$?

.... [1]

v What is the general formula for the alkane series? .... [1]

[Total: 18]

15 Organic 2

Extended

1 Butanol is the fourth member of the alcohols and has a molecular formula C_4H_9OH. Biobutanol is a fuel of the future. It can be made by the fermentation of almost any form of biomass such as grain, straw or leaves.

a Draw the structural formula of butanol.

[1]

b Write a word and a balanced symbol equation for the complete combustion of butanol.

....

.... [4]

c Why is it important to develop these fuels, such as biobutanol, as alternatives to petroleum?

....

.... [2]

2 All alcoholic drinks contain ethanol (alcohol).

a Explain why alcoholic drinks go sour if left open for some time. Write a word and balanced chemical equation to help with your explanation.

....

....

....

.... [5]

b i Alcohols react with carboxylic acids to produce which type of compound? .... [1]

ii Give two uses of the type of substance you have named in part **i**.

.... [2]

3 The structure of the cholesterol molecule is shown below.

a What type of bonding is present in this molecule? .... [1]

b Which part of the molecule will react with:

i steam? .... [1]

ii ethanoic acid? .... [1]

c If an addition polymer was to be made with this cholesterol, which part of the molecule would be likely to react?

.... [1]

d If a condensation polymer like Terylene was to be made with this cholesterol, which part of the molecule would be likely to react?

.... [1]

4 a Starch can undergo a process called hydrolysis. Explain what you understand by the term *hydrolysis*.

....

.... [2]

b i The chart below represents the breaking down of starch and subsequent reactions of the products. Identify and give the formulae of substances **A** to **C**.

$$\text{Starch} \xrightarrow{\text{dilute acid}} \textbf{A} \xrightarrow{\text{yeast}} \textbf{B} + \text{Carbon dioxide}$$

$$\textbf{B} \xrightarrow{\substack{\text{acidified} \\ \text{potassium} \\ \text{dichromate(VI)}}} \textbf{C} + \text{Water}$$

....

.... [6]

ii What test could be used to identify substance **C**?

....

.... *[3]*

iii What type of reagent is potassium dichromate(vɪ)? .... *[1]*

iv A different substance will be produced instead of **A** if an enzyme is used in the first stage.
Name the different substance that would be produced if an enzyme was used.

.... *[1]*

v Name an enzyme that could be used instead of the dilute acid. .... *[1]*

5 a Name the polymerisation process that is used to make both nylon and Terylene.

.... *[1]*

b Name the starting materials for making:

i nylon .... *[2]*

ii Terylene. .... *[2]*

c Give the name and formula of the small molecule produced during the polymerisation
reactions used to produce both nylon and Terylene. .... *[2]*

d Give the name of the chemical link that holds together:

i nylon .... *[1]*

ii Terylene. .... *[1]*

e Give two uses for:

i nylon .... *[2]*

ii Terylene. .... *[2]*

f Explain the difference between the type of polymerisation you have named in part **a** and
addition polymerisation.

....

....

.... *[2]*

6   The amount of ethanoic acid in vinegar can be determined by carrying out a titration. The results below came from a titration of a vinegar solution with sodium hydroxide solution. The neutralisation reaction taking place is:

$$CH_3COOH(aq) + NaOH(aq) \rightarrow CH_3COONa(aq) + H_2O(l)$$

$25.00\,cm^3$ of vinegar was just neutralised by $20.00\,cm^3$ of a $0.10\,mol\,dm^{-3}$ sodium hydroxide solution. Calculate:

a   the concentration of ethanoic acid in the vinegar solution

....

....

.... [3]

b   the mass of ethanoic acid in a 1 litre ($1\,dm^3$) bottle of this vinegar. (A_r values: H = 1; C = 12; O = 16)

....

....

.... [2]

7   a   Amino acids are essential for the formation of proteins. How many amino acids are there?

.... [1]

   b   Each amino acid contains two functional groups. What are the names of these functional groups?

.... [2]

   c   The structure of the first amino acid, glycine, is shown below.

      Redraw the structure to show a bonding diagram for this substance, showing the outer electron energy levels only.

[10]

d Amino acids are the building blocks for proteins. Proteins are long-chain molecules or natural polymers.

   i Name the polymerisation process that is required to form proteins.

....

                                                                           [1]

   ii Which industrial polymer contains the same link as that found in proteins?

....

                                                                           [1]

   iii The diagram below shows a dipeptide.

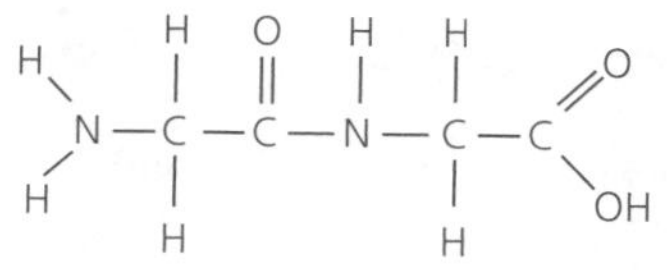

What do you understand by the term *dipeptide*?

.... *[1]*

   iv Draw a circle around the link that holds this dipeptide together. *[1]*

Exam focus

Core/Extended

1 Ethanol (alcohol) is a product of many fermentation reactions and of the hydration of ethene. The molecular formula of ethanol is C_2H_5OH.

  a Draw the structural formula of ethanol.

[1]

  b i Balance the following chemical equation for the fermentation reaction. Some spaces may be left blank.

      ....$C_6H_{12}O_6$(aq) → ....C_2H_5OH(l) + ...CO_2(g)   *[2]*

    ii Name the substance $C_6H_{12}O_6$. .... *[1]*

    iii Calculate the M_r value for $C_6H_{12}O_6$.

      .... *[1]*

c When ethanol is heated with potassium dichromate(vi), it is converted to ethanoic acid.

$C_2H_5OH(l) \rightarrow CH_3COOH(l)$

i   What type of reaction is this? .... [1]

ii Ethanoic acid belongs to a homologous series of organic acids. What is the name given to this homologous series of acids? .... [1]

iii When ethanoic acid is reacted with ethanol in the presence of a catalyst, a new substance is produced. Give the name and formula of this new substance.

.... [2]

iv Name the catalyst you would use for the reaction in part **iii**. .... [1]

v   The reaction in part **iii** is known as a reversible reaction. Explain the meaning of the term *reversible reaction*.

.... [1]

[*Total: 11*]

● Extended

2 The first member of the homologous series of carboxylic acids is methanoic acid (HCOOH).

a What do you understand by the term *homologous series*?

....

....

.... [5]

b In some areas, when water is boiled the inside of the kettle becomes coated with a layer of calcium carbonate. This type of water is known as temporary hard water. This deposit of calcium carbonate can be removed by adding methanoic acid.

i   Complete the equation for the reaction between calcium carbonate and methanoic acid.

$CaCO_3$ + ... $HCOOH \rightarrow Ca(HCOO)_2$ + ... + ... [3]

ii Methanoic acid reacts with most metals above hydrogen in the reactivity series.

Complete the word equation for the reaction between methanoic acid and magnesium.

methanoic acid + magnesium → .... + ... [2]

iii Aluminium is also above hydrogen in the reactivity series. Why do you think methanoic acid does not react with aluminium?

....

.... [1]

c Give the name, molecular formula and empirical formula of the third acid in this series.

.... [3]

[*Total: 14*]

16 Experimental chemistry

1 Concentrated sodium chloride solution was broken down by the passage of electricity using the apparatus shown below.

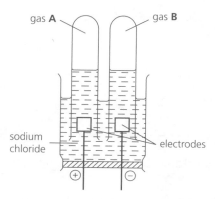

a What is the name of this process? .... [1]

b Suggest a suitable material from which to make the electrodes. .... [1]

c Gas A bleached moist indicator paper. What is gas A and what is its formula?

   .... [2]

d Gas B is hydrogen. Suggest a chemical test to prove this.

   ....

   .... [2]

2 Ethene can be obtained by passing liquid paraffin vapour over hot aluminium oxide or broken pot.

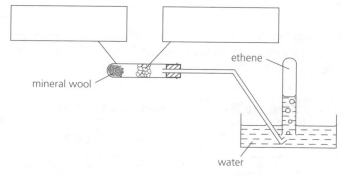

a Complete the boxes in the diagram to show the chemicals used in this experiment. [2]

b Show on the diagram where the heat is applied during the experiment using two arrows. [2]

c Why must the delivery tube be removed from the water before the heating is stopped?

   .... [1]

d Ethene is an unsaturated hydrocarbon. Describe a chemical test you could use to test for this unsaturation.

   ....

   .... [2]

3 A solid fertiliser for household plants is thought to contain both potassium ions and ammonium ions. Describe the tests that could be carried out to decide if this is the case.

....

....

....

....

....

.... [6]

4 In each of the qualitative analysis stages below, identify by name and formula the substances **A** to **E**.

a When blue-green crystals, **A**, were heated in a dry test-tube, a brown gas, **B**, was produced.

....

.... [4]

b A black solid residue, **C**, was left behind. When some dilute sulfuric acid was added to the black residue, the residue dissolved. There was no effervescence and a blue solution, **D**, was produced.

....

.... [4]

c Upon adding a few drops of barium chloride solution to a portion of **D**, a white precipitate, **E**, is formed, which is insoluble in dilute hydrochloric acid.

.... [2]

5 An analytical chemist was asked to identify two colourless solutions, **A** and **B**, and a green solid, **C**. He carried out various tests in an attempt to identify the solutions. The results of his tests are shown in the table below.

Substance	Flame test colour	Dilute HCl(aq)	Addition of NH_3(aq)		Dilute HNO_3(aq) + $AgNO_3$(aq)	Dilute HCl(aq) + $BaCl_2$(aq)
			Few drops	Excess		
A	Brick red	No reaction	White precipitate	Precipitate dissolves	White precipitate	No reaction
B	Lilac	No reaction	No reaction	No reaction	No reaction	White precipitate
C	Green	Fizzes	Blue precipitate when added to solution from effect of HCl(aq)	Precipitate dissolves	Fizzes	Fizzes

a Look at the results that were obtained for solution **A**.

i Which metal ion is present in the solution? .... [1]